GUIDE TO THE PRACTICAL STUDY OF HARMONY

GUIDE TO THE PRACTICAL STUDY OF HARMONY

Peter Ilyitch Tchaikovsky

DOVER PUBLICATIONS, INC.
Mineola, New York

Bibliographical Note

This Dover edition, first published in 2005, is an unabridged republication of the edition originally published by P. Jurgenson, Leipzig, in 1900.

International Standard Book Number: 0-486-44272-1

Manufactured in the United States of America
Dover Publications, Inc., 31 East 2nd Street, Mineola, N.Y. 11501

GUIDE

TO THE PRACTICAL STUDY

O F

HARMONY

B Y

P. Tschaikowsky

FORMER PROFESSOR AT THE IMPERIAL CONSERVATORY
OF MOSCOW.

Translated from the german version of P. Juon

b y

Emil Krall and James Liebling.

LEIPSIC,

P. Jurgenson.

19, Thalstrasse.

Moscow, P. Jurgenson.

Copyright by P. Jurgenson, Leipsic 1900.

Price: 3/— net.

TABLE OF CONTENTS.

HARMONY.

FIRST PART.

FIRST SECTION.

SECOND SECTION.

THIRD SECTION.

SECOND PART.

FIRST SECTION.

SECOND SECTION.

INTRODUCTION.

Intervals.

While it must be supposed, that the elements of musical science are familiar to everyone about to take up the art of composition, I deem it advisable to preface my treatise on Harmony with a short review of the subject of—*Intervals,*—as any uncertain conceptions on this ground might easily prove a hindrance to a thorough knowledge of Harmony.

The term „Interval“ represents the mutual relation of the tones with regard to their position in the scale. The lower tone of an interval is called the—*fundamental tone.*—The names of the intervals have their derivation in the Latin Ordinals, designating numerically the steps between fundamental tone and upper tone.

The raising or lowering of a tone of an interval causes no change in its name, while the distance between the two tones is widened or shortened.

To obtain a clear view of such alterations of intervals, we will arrange the latter into two groups:

I group comprising: *large* (major), *small* (minor), *augmented* and *diminished* intervals; (to which belong Seconds, Thirds, Sixths and Sevenths).

II group comprising: *perfect, augmented* and *diminished* intervals; (to which belong: Primes, Octaves, Fifths and Fourths).

Minor intervals are half a tone smaller than major intervals; augmented intervals are half a tone larger than either major or perfect ones; while diminished intervals are half a tone smaller than minor or perfect intervals.

All intervals having for their fundamental tone the first degree of the major scale are either major or perfect.

Let us now ascertain the number of whole and semi-tones contained in each of these intervals, thus establishing a scale or medium of comparison for all intervals:

A major	Second	contains:	one	whole tone	
„ „	Third	„	2	„	tones
„ pure	Fourth	„	2¹/₂	tones	
„ „	Fifth	„	3¹/₂	„	
„ major	Sixth	„	4¹/₂	„	
„ „	Seventh	„	5¹/₂	„	
„ pure	Octave	„	6	„	
„ „	Prime	„	0	„	

Having then obtained a knowledge of the various kinds of intervals and the means of gauging them, we are enabled to constitute exactly any relation between two given tones.

To illustrate the aforesaid, we will construct a table of all the intervals having C for their fundamental tone.

Thus we learn, that a major or a pure Interval is converted into a minor, diminished or augmented Interval by lowering or raising the upper tone—or, the latter remaining unchanged, by raising or lowering the fundamental tone. For instance:

Intervals exceeding the octave are but repetitions of the relations existing within the limits of an octave; the „Ninth“ alone has an independant significance in harmony.

*) The letter „C“ designates the intervals available in Harmony.

The *inversion* of Intervals is effected by transposing the upper tone into the octave below or the fundamental tone into the octave above. The relations thus arising may be expressed by the following figures:

1	2	3	4	5	6	7	8
8	7	6	5	4	3	2	1

The inverted Prime becomes an Octave, the Second a Seventh, the Third a Sixth, the Fourth a Fifth, the Fifth a Fourth, the Sixth a Third, the Seventh a Second, the Octave a Prime.

Major intervals become minor, while minor intervals become major; augmented intervals become diminished, diminished intervals augmented; pure intervals however remain pure.

According to the manner in which they affect the ear, intervals are separated into *Consonances* and *Dissonances*. The former are complete in themselves, as they express a certain *repose;* the latter, however, convey the element of *motion* and demand a goal or solution in the following interval.

Pure Primes, Octaves and Fifths as well as major and minor Thirds and Sixths are consonances, the first three being termed *perfect consonances*, and the major and minor Thirds and Sixths *imperfect consonances*. Seconds, Sevenths and all augmented and diminished intervals are dissonances. The pure Fourth partakes of the nature of both consonance and dissonance, inclining rather to the latter class.

HARMONY.

§ 1. Musical tones are combined in two different ways: first by allowing them to sound *separately* one after the other, then again by subjecting them to a *simultaneous concordance*. The first combination is named „Melody“, the second „Harmony“.

These two elements, together with the element of rythm, (which regulates them in their relation to the time or measure) constitute the Material of the art of music. The subject of this treatise shall be the simultaneous concordance of tones: Harmony.

First Part.

§ 2. The simultaneous sounding of three, four or five tones, separated from one another by the interval of a third, is called a *chord*. The simplest and at the same time most important chord is the *Triad*, which, as its name indicates, consists of three tones. Being composed of two consonant intervals (Third and Fifth) its effect on the musical ear is satisfying, in contrast to that of chords consisting of four or five tones, which contain dissonant intervals and hence cannot appear independently, but must be supported by or resolved into a consonating chord or triad.

First Section.

Consonant chords.—Triads.

§ 3. The triad, or common chord consists of three tones, separated each from the other by the interval of a Third.

The lowest tone is called: *Fundamental tone,* or *Base*—the intermediate tone: the *Third*—and the highest tone: the *Fifth* of the triad. Triads are divided, according to the kinds of Thirds and Fifths that compose them. A large or *major triad* is a chord composed of a major Third and a perfect Fifth (a). Minor Third and perfect Fifth constitute a *minor triad* (b); minor Third and diminished Fifth a *diminished triad* (c).

CHAPTER I.

The Triads of the Major Scale.

§ 4. If we construct a triad on each successive degree of the diatonic major scale, we obtain the following chords:

On the 1-st, 4-th and 5-th degree we find major triads:

These triads. representing the most essential constituents of the major scale, bear the names of those degrees of the scale, on which they are based.

The triad on the 1-st degree is termed the Tonic triad
„ „ „ „ 4-th „ „ „ „ Subdominant triad
„ „ „ „ 5-th „ „ „ „ Dominant triad

§ 5. It has just been said that these three major triads form the most essential constituents of the major scale. Verily they contain all the diatonic degrees of the scale; and, being most closely related to one another, they indicate clearly and unmistakeably the key and further suffice for the harmonic accompaniment of any melody that does not surpass the limits of the key in question. Their mutual affinity is easily demonstrated by the degree of relation existing between the several scales to which they belong. The triads on the 4-th and 5-th degrees, while they are respectively the Subdominant and Dominant in the harmony of the given key, are at the same time the *tonic* triads of those keys, which, in the so-called „Circle of Fifths" are nearest to the given key. *So that the inner relationship of the three major triads in the harmony of the major scale is in direct proportion to the degree of relationship of the three successive keys in the Circle of Fifths (their Tetrachords being common).*

§ 6. In the major scale minor triads are also found, namely on the 2-nd, 3-rd and 6-th degrees. The minor Third imparts to these triads a soft, weakened character, hence they cannot command the importance possessed by the major triads. However, they furnish us with a beautiful contrast to the latter, emphasizing their strength! Their mutual affinity is the same as that of the major triads, as they possess the same proximity in the Circle of Fifths.

Of the degree of their relationship to the major triads we may say it is the same as that existing between parallel keys; for the chords on the 1-st and 6-th degrees, the 5-th and 3-rd degree and the 4-th and 2-nd degree respectively are separated by a minor third.

The whole mass of major and minor triads may be grouped into three sets of two triads each:

a) The tonic group viz: the triads on the 1-st and 6-th degrees.

b) The dominant group viz: the triads on the 5-th and 3-rd degrees and

c) The subdominant group viz: the triads on the 1-th and 2-nd degrees.

§ 7. In marked contrast to the other triads stands the diminished triad on the 7-th degree, because of its dissonant character. We shall return to this chord later on, having first entirely mastered the connection of the other six triads.

CHAPTER II.

The Connection of the Triads of the major scale.

§ 8. In music chords are either used in masses, that is with manifold repetitions of one and the same interval—as is the case in compositions for orchestra and Pianoforte—or they are set for several, single, distinct voices. „Four-voiced-writing" is the commonest and most normal form, as it denotes the four different human voices—namely: *Soprano, Alto, Tenor* and *Bass*. So, in our study of Harmony we shall keep to this disposition of the voices.

The highest voice—Soprano—and the deepest voice—Bass—are called the two *outer voices*—the two intermediate voices: Alto and Tenor: the two *inner voices*.

§ 9. Turning now to the practical application of the above treated chords, we will begin with placing the fundamental tone in the Bass. In the highest voice any of the three tones of the chord, the fundamental tone, the Third or the Fifth may be used. For the two inner voices we will use respectively the intervals of the triad nearest to the Soprano. The C major triad would thus appear as follows:

These three cases are called the *positions* of the chord. According to the interval of the triad which appears in the Soprano, these positions are called the fundamental position or position of the octave, the position of the Third, and the position of the Fifth.

§ 10. From the above example we see that in each of the three positions the fundamental tone is used twice, while the third and fifth appear but once. Shall this always be the case? By no means! In a free leading of the voices the composer may double any tone of the chord at will. For the present, however, we cannot avail ourselves of this liberty, since according to § 9—we must place the inner voices as close as possible to the upper voice. Indeed, the doubling of the fundamental tone will always be the most common, as it is most natural to the triad *).

---

*) This is confirmed by the so called natural scale, which exhibits but two Fifths and one Third against three fundamental tones.

§ 11. We have already mentioned (§ 6) the internal relationship of the triads of the scale. Now, there is still another and purely external connection of these triads, growing out of the tones they have in common. The triads c, e, g and g, b, d for instance have the tone g in common, while the triad f, a, c shares the tone c with the triad c, e, g. In fact each triad has one or two tones in common with every other triad constructed on steps of the same scale, except in the case where the fundamentals are directly succeeding steps. So: the triad on C has no tone in common with the triads on b. and d; the triad on d. none with the triads on c and e, and so on. The mutual relationship of the triads with regard to their external connection is shown in the following table:

$$
\begin{array}{lll}
*_1 \quad \left\{\begin{array}{l}G\\F\end{array}\right. & C\leftarrow\rightarrow\left\{\begin{array}{l}C\\e\\d\end{array}\right. & F\leftarrow\rightarrow\left\{\begin{array}{l}C\\d\\a\end{array}\right. \\
C\rightarrow\left\{\begin{array}{l}a\\e\end{array}\right. & & \\
a\leftarrow\rightarrow\left\{\begin{array}{l}C\\F\\e\\d\end{array}\right. & c\leftarrow\rightarrow\left\{\begin{array}{l}G\\C\\a\end{array}\right. & d\leftarrow\rightarrow\left\{\begin{array}{l}F\\G\\a\end{array}\right.
\end{array}
$$

To effect a connection of two triads at once correct and satisfying to the ear, it is nessary to retain the common tone of the triads in the same voice.

Conscientious application of this rule imparts fluency, euphony and unity to the harmony; moreover it enables the pupil to avoid many grave errors, which, otherwise, he would of necessity commit. Take for instance the triad on c in the octave position, and let us connect it successively with other triads containing tones in common with it. Which positions of the new chords must we then choose? Obviously those which enable us to retain the common tone, or tones in the same voice. Consequently the G major triad must appear in position of the third, F major in the position of the fifth, A minor in position of the third and E minor again in position of the fifth.

The progression and position, therefore, of the three upper voices is influenced by the common tones. Meanwhile the Bass may progress upward or downward at liberty. Should we have to choose between a skip of a sixth and one of a third, we prefer the latter **).

---

*) The major triads are indicated by Capital, minor triads by small letters.

**) Having a purely practical aim in this work, we shall avoid minute explanations and justifications of the different rules. It were well for the pupil to search out instinctively, as it were, the justification of the several rules. For this purpose he should thoroughly test them by ear on the piano. A true musical instinct will at once convince him, that all these rules originated in the demands of his own ear.

Examples.

I Remark. In addition to these examples, which consist in supplying the remaining three voices to a given bass, it is very beneficial to construct a table, which shall contain all the possible connections of all triads with one another, in every position. To this end the example (№ 13) begun in this paragraph on C should be carried on further. The pupil must not be disheartened, when he finds that at the very beginning of his study 120 chords must be written out in one key alone. In the first place the labor is merely a mechanical one, and in the second place it is important that by thoroughgoing explanations of the rudiments we should dispel at the start the superstitious awe that prevails regarding the so-called „Theory" or „Thorough Bass".

II. Remark: In harmonizing a bass, care should be taken not to lead the voices too high; therefore one must not choose too high a position of the tonic triad at the start.

CHAPTER III.

Connection of Triads, showing no external agreement.

§ 12. In the preceding chapter we spoke of the beauty of harmonies connected by common tones. This absolute completeness in chord-connection, however. does not exclude the admissibility of certain connections, which, while perhaps less pleasing, satisfy us by very reason of their sharpness or coarseness. This we can understand if we consider the aim of Music, which is, to picture the many various emotions of the soul: and these cannot always be expressed by dulcet soothing means. For this reason Harmony admits also such chord-connections, which show no outer relationship— though they may bear an inner relationship to one another. (§ 5).

§ 13. Should we not, when connecting two chords not outwardly related chose again those positions, that permit a melodious, fluent leading of the voices? Should we not, to avoid jumps, lead each voice into the nearest interval, a second up or down? For instance as follows:

16.

Before answering these questions, however, let us see, what different kinds of voice-motions there are.

We perceive the three following kinds:

1) *Parallel motion* (motus rectus), in which two voices progress in one and the same direction, that is, upwards or downwards.

17.

2) *Oblique motion* (motus obliquus), in which one voice remains stationary, while the other moves onward:

18.

3) *Contrary motion* (motus contrarius); one voice progresses upwards, the other downwards.

19.

All these various motions are admissible in every succession of harmonies. Observe, however, the so called *Parallelisms* occurring in the motus rectus; these are progressions, in which the two voices move not only in the same direction, but also in the same interval; for instance: when two voices progress upward or downward in Seconds or Fourths.

Some of these Parallelisms are indeed very euphonious and, therefore, like the other motions, entirely permissible. Others, however, are to be avoided partly because they do not satisfy the musical ear and again, because they counteract the independent movement of the voices. Such forbidden progressions are *Parallel Fifths and Octaves*.

Remark. To comprehend clearly the reason for prohibiting parallel Fifths and Octaves, it must be borne in mind that we have to deal not with the massive harmonization of orchestra or piano composition, but with 4 separate independent voices, which do not permit of extensive doubling. Should the question arise whether only parallel octaves and fifths are forbidden, and parallel dissonant intervals permitted, we may add, that for the present we are familiar only with tone-combinations, in which such progressions do not occur. Once for all, then, let it be said that in Harmony progressions of parallel fifths and octaves are prohibited.

Now only are we in a position to answer the question put at the beginning of this paragraph.

If we wish to connect two triads having no external relationship, we can not lead all the voices a second upwards or downwards, as parallel fifths and octaves would arise.

To avoid this fault we must employ contrary motion, without, however, proceeding in great skips.

The fault is by no means corrected, if we replace the step of a second by a skip of a seventh in the opposite direction (contrary motion), as in that case the fifths and octaves really remain.

Moreover, we obtain a very unmelodious skip of a seventh in the Bass.

So we will allow the Bass to retain its melodious step of a second, and, employing contrary motion, lead each of the other voices into the nearest interval of the following chord.

24.

We have now learned, how to connect, within its own limits, all the consonant chords of the major scale in all positions. Besides working out the following written exercises, we chould advise the pupil to form at the piano all manners of chord-combinations in all the keys, in order to master them more thoroughly.

Exercises.

25

CHAPTER IV.

Deviations from rules governing the connection of related triads.

§ 14. In the foregoing exercises we retained the common tone in the same voice, when connecting two chords and thus obtained greater beauty and smoothness in harmonic progressions. We need observe this rule, however, only in so far as it does not hinder us in our true purpose: a free and independent leading of the voices.

This aim we will seek gradually to attain by disregarding at times those restraining rules, whose purpose it was at the start to fortify us against error. Even at this stage we might occasionally do so, provided we thereby improve the voice-leading. Thus it has been said, for example, that the position of the upper voices should not be too high. Now, if we see that this can be avoided by a deviation from the rule in question, we may make such a deviation, observing, however, the necessary precaution. We must bear in mind chiefly the following points:

1) Two triads, however closely related internally and externally, must never directly follow each other in the same position, as parallel fifths and octaves must necessarily occur.

2) The uppermost voice must make no jumps greater than a fourth.

3) In this case the Bass must progress in contrary motion to the upper parts, so that no *concealed* Fifths and Octaves are formed.

Besides the parallel or open Fifths and Octaves there exist also concealed ones. These occur, when two voices jump in parallel motion into a Fifth or Octave.

These hidden progressions, however, lose their disagreeable nature, if the two chords possess a common tone, which remains in the same voice, e. g.

But if this rule is not applied, the concealed Fifths and Octaves sound extremely unpleasant.

Directly we employ contrary motion, which excludes these hidden progressions, the same chord-combinations sound pleasant.

31.

In the following examples therefore, deviations from the rule in question are admissible only, if contrary motion can be employed in the Bass.

If the leading tone, the third of the Dominant triad, is in the Soprano voice, and the Dominant triad is followed by the tonic, the deviation is not permitted, as the tendency of the leading tone is to move upward a half-tone into the tonic. Should we find it, however, in one of the inner voices, we may lead it a third downward.

not good.   good.   good.

32.

The same holds good for the tonic triad, if succeeded by the sub-dominant triad. In this case the third of the tonic triad partakes of the nature of the leading tone, since these two chords have the same relationship as Dominant to Tonic.

33.

Exercises.

34.

CHAPTER V.

Harmonic Sequences.

§ 15. A *Harmonic Sequence* is a chord-progression, in which a motive consisting of two or more chords is repeated a number of times, always on different steps of the scale, thereby giving rise to motion downwards or upwards.

In the repetitions the same arrangement of voices has to prevail as in the motive.

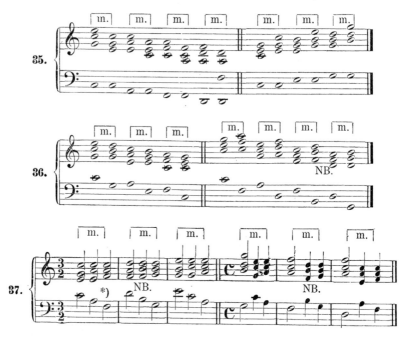

The motive may consist either of several positions of one and the same chord, or of different chords properly connected.

§ 16. At the places marked NB. we find the diminished triad on the 7-th degree. Because of the dissonant interval it contains (the diminished fifth) it must not be used with as much liberty as the other triads of the scale. We will, therefore, indulge in its use only with the greatest precaution. Its use in the Sequence is justified on the ground that the repetition of the motive and the carrying out of the Sequence demand it.

§ 17. It may be stated with regard to the diminished triad, that its use is not absolutely restricted to the Sequence. It may appear, for instance, supported between two related triads, in which case the common tones must unquestionably be retained in the same voices.

---

*) Contrary to the rule in § 11. the Bass here progresses upward by a Sixth, instead of downward by a Third. This is permitted whenever the carrying out of the motive demands it.

Exercises *).

CHAPTER VI.

The Harmony of the minor scale.

§ 18. The Harmony of the minor scale is built up on the so-called „*harmonic minor scale*" and consists of the same notes as its parallel major scale, with the exception that the 7-th step is raised by half a tone. This is done in order to establish a *leading-tone*, which, as the pupil will perceive later, is indispensable to the *cadence* **). Hence arises the characteristic interval of

---

*) At the bracketed places sequences are to be constructed as in the examples.
**) Each composition is closed by a *cadence*, which consists of the Dominant triad and the tonic. We refer to it later on.

the minor scale; namely the augmented second between the 6-th and 7-th steps,

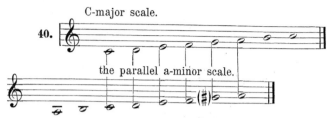

The other minor scale—called the *melodic*, has no significance in Harmony; for as its name implies, it is merely a melodic variation of the harmonic scale, made in order to avoid the dissonant step of the augmented second.

§ 19. If we construct triads on the steps of the minor-scale, we obtain only four consonant chords: two small or minor triads (on the tonic and sub-dominant) and two great or major triads (on the dominant and the 6-th step).

In the remaining triads we find dissonant intervals'—diminished or augmented Fifths.

Since, as we have remarked before, the real essence of harmony lies in chords that are euphonious, complete in themselves and consonant, there is no need of demonstrating that the harmony of the minor-scale is not so rich in material as that of the major.

§ 20. In connecting the consonant triads in minor we will follow the rules laid down in the preceding chapter. Regarding the use in minor of the two diminished triads on the 2-nd and 7-th degree and the augmented triad (so-called, because of its augmented fifth) on the third degree, we must first make several observations.

We know that a dissonant chord demands support, which may consist either in a correct outward connection with its two neighbouring triads, or in its internal relationship to them—as in the carrying out of a motive (e. g. in a sequence).

Since, however, harmonic sequences, which justify the use of the diminished triad in major, are not quite practicable in minor because of the many dissonant chords, let us see, if diminished and augmented triads cannot be used otherwhere than in a sequence, perhaps by invariably placing them between two consonant chords.

1. *The diminished triad on the 7-th degree* is related to the triads on the 2-nd, 4-th and 5-th degrees; still it can be properly connected only with the Dominant triad, as the connection with the other two would call for a step of an augmented second, which sounds very unpleasant and is always to be avoided.

43.

This triad then can be connected only with the Dominant triad, the two common tones being kept in the same voices.

44.

This succession of chords—it must be observed—while being possible, is extremely rare.

II. *The diminished triad on the 2-nd degree* can be connected with the triads on the 4-th, 5-th and 6-th degree. Avoid however:

a) concealed Octaves and Fifths

b) the step of the augmented second.

The latter disappears, if, in connecting the diminished with the dominant triad, contrary motion is employed.

45.

III. *The augmented triad* (on the 3-rd degree) can without difficulty be connected with the triads on the 1-st, 5-th and 6-th degrees. This triad is but seldom used as a diatonic chord; as a chromatic or altered chord, however, it is much applied—as we shall see later on.

46.

§ 21. In the preceding paragraph it was remarked, that the step of the augmented second should be avoided at all times. For this reason the leading-tone (third of the dominant triad) is led upwards in joining the triads on the 5-th and 6-th degrees. The triad on the 6-th degree then appears with doubled third and an arrangement of the voices, which deviates from the general rule.

47.

When these two triads succeed each other in opposite order to the above, which indeed seldom occurs, the third of the triad on the 6-th degree must be doubled for the same reason.

Exercises.

Remark. The figures and accidentals below the notes in these examples are the signs of the so-called *figured Bass*. These signs, which indicate the Harmony, are placed above or below the Bass—notes. In this connection observe the following rules:

a) The triads in their fundamental form (others are unknown to us for the present) are designated by figures corresponding to their intervals: $3, 5, 8; \begin{smallmatrix}3\\5\end{smallmatrix}; \begin{smallmatrix}3\\5\\8\end{smallmatrix}$. Except in a few cases these figures are not employed; so that bass-notes without figures below them signify the fundamental form of the triad. Single figures as 3, 5, 8, refer to the position of the triad:

50.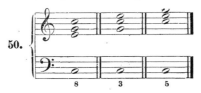

b) Accidentals not occurring in the signature of the key, as well as naturals must invariably be given in figured—Bass. Note here, that an accidental unaccompanied by any figure always refers to the third of the chord. Should the accidental be meant for a different interval, the figure designating that interval must be placed to the right of the accidental.

Accordingly the accidental referring to the third of the dominant triads in the above bass are unaccompanied by any figure:

51.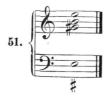

while the accidental referring to the fifth of the augmented triad has the figure 5 next to it:

52.

CHAPTER VII.

Open Position.

§ 22. A distribution of the voices, in which, reckoning down from the Soprano, the Alto and Tenor have respectively the next succeeding intervals, is called „close position".

In distinction to this we have the „open position"; in which the inner voices are separated from the Soprano and from each other by two intervals of the chord, so that what was Tenor in close position becomes Alto in open, and the tone that served for Alto is transposed down an octave into the Tenor. So one and the same group of chords can be written in two different ways.

Close Position.

53.

Open Position.

54.

A merely mechanical transposition of the inner voices, however, makes it evident that our leading of the voices is by no means free as yet; that, in other words, the inner voices are still subordinate to the upper voice. While the voices are, in most cases, distributed to best advantage in either of these two positions—which we shall call *normal* positions—we call attention to the fact that, the freer and more independent the movement of the voices, the more beautiful the harmony. Each voice must be independent of the others. Neither close nor open positions must preponderate; they must alternate and even give way to still other—exceptional positions.

Exercises: It will suffice, to work out the foregoing exercises in open position.

<h1 style="text-align:center">CHAPTER VIII.</h1>

<h2 style="text-align:center">The Inversions of the Triad.</h2>

§ 23. The fundamental tone of a triad is not always in the Bass, it may be substituted by the third or the fifth of the triad.

A triad, which has not the fundamental tone for its Bass is called *inverted;* and the process by which the fundamental is transposed into one of the upper voices is called „*Inversion*" of the triad.

Every triad has two inversions:

55.

The first inversion is called the *chord of the third and sixth,* because the upper voices are distant respectively a third and a sixth from the Bass. This chord is more briefly called the *chord of the sixth.*

The second inversion is called the *chord of the sixth and fourth.*

Beside the external distinction between the fundamental triad and its inversions, there exists an internal, or, we might say, „*spiritual*" difference. This latter is evinced by the different harmonic significance of these three forms of the triad, as well as by their different impressions on the human ear.

The triad in its fundamental form contains a perfect consonance — the pure Fifth—which lends to it the element of absolute repose and completeness in itself. This chord is perfect, an „accord parfait", as the French call it. The inversions of the triad, however, contain no perfect consonances; they lack this element of repose and evince a tendency to progress. For this reason the inversions of the triads are—as a rule—to be found in the middle of a composition, rarely at the commencement, and never at the end.

The manipulation of the inversions of the triads will present some difficulties to the student. But these he will doubtless overcome with the aid of rules serving that purpose. The rules, however, will be disclosed to him later on, in the harmonization of given melodies.

§ 24. Hitherto we have doubled only the fundamental tone in the fundamental form of the triad. We remarked, it will be remembered, that this is not only the most usual, but also the best course to pursue, as the nature of the chord seems to demand if. If, now, we distribute the upper voices of the inversions in the same manner as in the fundamental position, we obtain the following aspects of the chord:

In the chord of the sixth the third appears doubled; in the chord of the six-four—the fifth. A doubling of the third, however, being unnatural and unsatisfactory to the musical ear, it is better to double the fundamental tone or the fifth in the chord of the sixth. This necessitates an exceptional position of the voices.

The advisibility of doubling any one interval depends on the distribution of the voices in the preceding chord, or on the connection of the chord of the sixth with the following chord.

The doubling of the third in the chord of the sixth is by no means prohibited, if it can be justified by good voice-leading.

59.

Remark. Frequently we meet with a whole series of chords of the sixth, which follow scalewise one after the other. In such a case it is best to lead two voices parallel to the Bass and the third in contrary motion to it. Thus we obtain an alternate doubling of fundamental, third and fifth. If the Bass moves upward, we commence by doubling the Fifth; if downward, we double first the fundamental.

60.

If the chord of the sixth of the dominant triad is followed by the tonic, the third of the former must never be doubled, as it is the leading tone.

61.

A doubled fifth sounds not at all unpleasant; so that the close position of the upper voices of the six-four chord may be retained. The fundamental is doubled only in cases where we wish to avoid concealed octaves, which sound especially bad in the six-four chord.

62.

§ 25. The chord of the sixth will be discoursed at length later on; for the present we can say that it appears much more seldom than the other

forms of the triad. It assumes great importance, however, in a certain harmonic closing formula, called the „Cadence".

Exercises.

Note 1. The inversions of triads are figured according to their names.
the first—6; the second—$\frac{4}{6}$.

Note 11. The pupil must take the greatest pains to avoid forbidden
progressions, as only the most unplagging attention serves eventually to
eliminate them entirely. For this purpose the position of the chords must
frequently be changed. If for instance in the last two bars of the 4-th exercise the triad on G be placed in the position of the third and the voices
led respectively into the nearest intervals of the following chords, we obtain
three successive parallel fifths:

We avoid these faulty progressions, however, by placing the triad on G in the position of the fifth:

65.

As regards concealed progressions, we would say that, while they are if possible to be avoided, they are not absolutely forbidden, if the leading of the voices demands them. The concealed octaves, for instance, which appear in the following sequence, are pretty well justified by the repetition of the motive:

(the 5-th bar of the 3-rd exercise)

66.

Much more to be condemned would be their appearance in the motive itself instead of in its repetition:

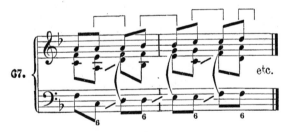

67.

In working these exercises the pupil will meet with numerous little obstacles, which theory is not able to point out; but these will gradually disappear, as the pupil strives to perfect his technic.

CHAPTER IX.

The Inversions of the Diminished and Augmented Triads.

§ 26. The first inversion of the diminished triad is of great significance in Harmony, and is, unlike the inversions of other triads, even more in use than its fundamental form. The reason for this is that the chord of the sixth of the diminished triad is in reality a consonant chord, its upper voices forming respectively a third and a sixth with the Bass. The fundamental form of this triad on the other hand, contains a diminished fifth and therefore belongs to the dissonant chords. The second inversion sounds exceedingly harsh aud is therefore hardly ever used, except in three-part-writing.

§ 27. In connecting the chord of the sixth of the diminished triad with other triads of the key the following two cases should be distinguished:

1) when it precedes the tonic triad.

2) when it precedes another triad of the scale.

In the first case the fundamental tone of the triad is at the same time leading tone and must be led upward, for which reason it must not be doubled. The best tone to double here would be the fifth, though occasionally the third is doubled.

68.

As the leading tone must at all times resolve into the tonic, the fifth of the diminished triad must not move upward, when placed *above* the fundamental tone, since forbidden progressions would necessarily arise.

69.

For this reason we must always avoid in the said chord of the sixth a position of voices, in which two fifths appear above the fundamental tone:

70.

The connection of this chord with the tonic triad is very common.

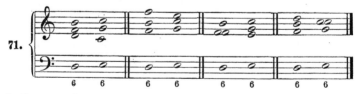

71.

In the second of the above mentioned cases, chiefly the fundamental tone—(as in all other chords of the sixth) is doubled, since it is no longer leading tone.

72.

The use of the chord of the sixth of the diminished triad on the second degree (in minor) is subject to the general rules.

§ 28. The inversions of the augmented triad on the 3-rd degree in minor present so many difficulties in their connection with other triads (even though related), that for the present we must abstain from using them; the more so, as we shall return to this chord later on, when we shall treat it as an incidental or passing harmony of the major scale.

Exercises.

Note: The signs occurring in the last three exercises are applied in accordance with the rules laid down in division b. of the note to § 21.

Second Section.

Dissonant Harmonies, Chords of the Seventh and Chords of the Ninth.

All chords consisting of four or five tones are dissonant chords, as their fundamental tone forms a seventh or a ninth with the uppermost tone. These chords are not independent harmonies. but find their support and justification in the chord that follows them. The leading of a dissonant into a consonant chord is called „resolution". Every chord of the seventh must be resolved into a triad.

CHAPTER X.

The Dominant Chord.

§ 29. If we superimpose an additional third on each triad of the diatonic scale, we obtain a series of chords of the seventh.

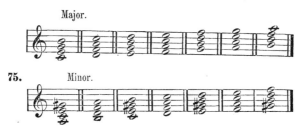

Of all these chords of the seventh, the most important and frequently used is that on the 5-th degree. It is called the *chord of the dominant-seventh,* or briefly, *dominant chord;* it resolves into the tonic triad.

The resolution is effected in the following manner: the seventh moves (like all dissonances) one degree downward; that is, into the third of the triad. The fifth progresses one degree upward or descends one degree into the third or the fundamental tone of the triad; more frequently into the latter. The third (here leading tone) progresses one degree upward, into the tonic; and the fundamental tone leaps upward a fourth or downward a fifth into the fundamental tone of the triad.

The resolution of the Dominant chord produces an incomplete form of the triad, in which the fifth is wanting. This is seen in the following examples.

In the Octave-position of the Dominant chord one interval must be omitted, as the doubling of the fundamental leaves but two voices for the remaining three intervals (third, fifth and seventh). In most cases the fifth is dropped, its absence being least felt; on rare occasions the third is omitted.

In these examples the fundamental tone in the Bass was correctly resolved. So, the fundamental tone in the upper voice cannot be resolved in the same way, lest parallel octaves are formed. It must therefore remain stationary—that is, resolve into the fifth of the triad. In this way the connection of the Dominant chord with the tonic triad becomes more emphonious and smooth, besides producing a complete triad, in which the fifth is not wanting. With the same purpose in view the fifth of the dominant chord in the positions of the third and fifth is omitted and the fundamental tone doubled.

§ 30. The Dominant chord has three inversions:

The names of these inversions are derived from the intervals formed between the bass and one of the chief tones (seventh or fundamental of the dominant chord. Thus:

    the first inversion is called: *chord of the sixth and fifth*
    the second is called: *chord of the fourth and third*
    the third   „   „   *chord of the second.*

These inversions are resolved according to the rules set down in the last paragraph; with the one exception, that the fundamental tone, which lies in the upper or in one of the middle voices, always remains stationary, so that the resolution results in a perfect triad.

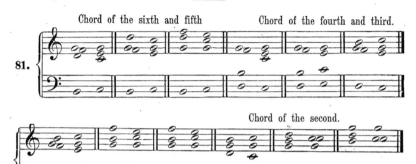

Chord of the sixth and fifth.   Chord of the fourth and third.

81.

Chord of the second.

In addition be it remarked, that the fifth of the dominant chord, whether in its fundamental form or in its inversions, is usually led downwards; only in cases where it appears necessary, it is led upwards, giving a triad with doubled third.

82.

As a preliminary exercise the pupil should write the Dominant chord in all its positions, with all possible resolutions, and in all keys; close and wide positions are to be employed in turn.

2-nd Exercises.

83.

Note. The figuring of the Dominant chord and its inversions is done according to their names. The fundamental form is expressed by the figure 7; the chord of the sixth and fifth by $\frac{6}{5}$; the chord of the sixth and fourth by $-\frac{4}{3}$; the chord of the second by 2.

In minor the necessary accidentals must appear; those relating to the third without an accompanying figure—as before mentioned—and those referring to other intervals of the chord with the appropriate figure.

APPENDIX TO CHAPTER X.

§ 30. Here we wish to point out some exceptions to the rules governing the resolution of the Dominant chord.

a) The Dominant chord resolves into the chord of the sixth, if the Bass leaps a third downward. In this case an exceptional resolution of the seventh is imperative, if we would avoid some extremely unpleasant concealed octaves.

b) The Dominant chord may also resolve into the six - four chord of the triad, if the Bass remains stationary. Where there are two fundamental tones, both of them must be retained in the same voice.

c) In the fundamental form of the Dominant chord the third may sometimes progress two steps downward and the seventh one step upward; but only in case these intervals lie in the inner voices. The Alto is best adapted to such progressions. Contrary motion must be used to avoid concealed fifths and octaves.

d) In the third inversion the fifth—when lying in the Soprano or Tenor voice—may leap a fourth upward, or a fifth downward. But faulty progressions, open or concealed, must be carefully avoided.

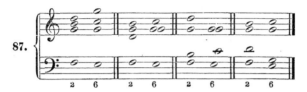

e) There are still several other deviations from the rules, in resolving the first two inversions of the Dominant chord; but they occur more rarely. As these have for their object a free leading of the voices, with which the pupil is not yet familiar, I will make but brief mention of them at this point, without recommending their employment.

§ 31. We have already mentioned that only the fundamental tone of the Dominant chord may be doubled. It may be added though, that, on rare occasions the fifth is omitted and the fundamental tone doubled, also in the chord of the sixth and fifth and of the second.

Exercises.

CHAPTER XI.

Free Voice-Leading.

§ 32. We have learnt that the voices of a chord may appear in close or open position; and that these two positions are the most normal and advantageous. But true harmonic beauty does not consist in arranging the voices of a chord in this way or that; in consists rather in the character and independence of the voices themselves—that is, in voice-leading which not only is not dependent on these two positions, but, on the contrary, gives rise to either one of them by reason of its peculiar character. Hitherto, in all our examples, the movement of the middle voices was determined by the upper voice and thus no opportunity for independence was offered. But as soon as it is no longer dominated by the upper voice, each voice gains in significance, deriving, as it were, a distinct physiognomy and character of its own, which entirely determines the positions of the voices in a chord; so that an arbitrary use of close or wide positions is not practicable. The alternate employment of these two positions will then be found necessary. A free leading of the voices may also occasion an exceptional or abnormal position of the intervals of a chord, as for instance in the following triad on C:

It should be remembered, then, that free voice-leading is of such a nature as to bring about not only an alternate recurrence of the two normal positions, but also accidental, unsymmetrical positions of the intervals.

§ 33. To gain a clear idea of the character of the several voices, we must remember in the first place, that we have to deal with *outer* and *inner* voices.

The two *outer* voices (Soprano and Bass) are of a very mobile nature. They might be likened to a curved line rising and falling in waves. Fifths and fourths are characteristic jumps in the Bass; though this voice is also very partial to scale—like progressions by steps, mostly in contrary motion to the Soprano.

The Soprano best adapts itself to progression by steps, though jumps of fourths, fifths, sixths and octaves are by no means excluded. Such jumps, however, must never follow one another in close succession.

The *inner* voices are distinctly averse to much motion; they are fitted by nature to retain the common tones of chords. Often they retain one and the same tone through two, three or more bars. The inner voices are best kept at an altitude not too high and should not be too far apart from each other. Where the chord is not in close position, however, they must not approach each other too closely. We must be peculiar to avoid a position of the voices, in which the inner voices are close to the Bass, with the Soprano lying very high. Theory can supply but a very general insight into the nature of the voices. It is for the student—provided he is sufficiently talented—gradually to learn and appreciate by diligent application all the finer points and peculiarities of free-voice-leading — matters which cannot be laid down in formula.

The following is an example of free-voice-leading:

Exercises: Work the foregoing exercises, beginning at chapter X, employing a free leading of the voices.

Note. In the exercises the pupil must not overstep the limits of the human voices represented respectively by the parts. These limits are as follows: *Soprano* from $\overline{\mathrm{d}}$ to $\overline{\overline{\mathrm{g}}}$: *Alto:* from the small $\overline{\mathrm{a}}$ to the $\overline{\overline{\mathrm{d}}}$; *Tenor:* from the small $\underline{\mathrm{d}}$ to the $\overline{\mathrm{g}}$; *Bass:* from the great, g to the $\overline{\mathrm{c}}$. Only in cases of absolute necessity can these limits be surpassed, and then never by more than one tone.

Exercises.

CHAPTER XII.

The chord of the Ninth.

§ 34. In major, as well as in minor we find on the 5-th degree a five—voiced chord: this is called *the chord of the ninth,* because of the interval of a ninth formed by the lowest voice and the uppermost voice.

This doubly - dissonant chord contains, in major, a major ninth, and is therefore called the *major chord of the ninth.* In minor it contains a minor ninth—and is called the *minor chord of the ninth.* The chord of the ninth resolves into the tonic triad; the intervals already discussed in the Dominant chord, are led as before; the ninth, however, progresses one degree downward—like the seventh.

In four-part-writing the *fifth* is omitted.

§ 35. The chord of the ninth, being a strongly dissonant chord, must be *prepared;* that is, the ninth must be part of the preceding chord, and must be kept in the same voice. The triads of the 2-nd, 4-th and 6-th degrees may serve as such preparing chords.

The tonic triad can also serve as preparing chord, if it appears in the same position as in the resolution of the chord of the ninth.

§ 36. Inversions of the chord of the ninth are not used.

Note. In figured Bass this chord is designated by 9.

*) The figures 8 7 denote that in the Dominant triad the octave should be led into the seventh, whereby the Dominant chord is formed.

CHAPTER XIII.

Chords of the minor and diminished seventh.

§ 37. Next in importance to the Dominant chord is the chord of the seventh on the 7-th degree of the scale. In major it is called: the chord of the minor seventh, in minor: chord of the diminished seventh.

minor, — dimin. sev. ch.

97.

As regards their resolution, these chords are treated as chords of the ninth without fundamental tone. Consequently their fundamental tone (the third of the chord of the ninth) is led one degree upward—their third (fifth of the chord of the ninth) one degree upward or downward—their fifth (formerly seventh) and seventh (formerly ninth) one degree downward. Should the third lie below the seventh, it cannot progress downwards, or parallel Fifths would be formed.

98.

§ 38. The inversions of these two chords of the seventh bear the same names as those of the Dominant chord.

Sixth and Fourth   Chord of the Fourth & Third   Second

99.

The fifth, (formerly seventh) if it lies in one of the middle-voices, may exceptionally be resolved upwards, provided no faulty progressions result.

Such a deviation is decidedly advantageous in the resolution of the chord of the second, as the voices of the resulting six - four chord derive thereby a normal position.

§ 39. The chord of the diminished seventh gains greatly by being prepared, though this is not absolutely necessary, as in the case of the minor seventh-chord.

The tonic triad may be used as preparation for this seventh-chord, if it appears in the same position in preparation and resolution. In the same way also the Dominant triad, as it has two tones in common with this seventh chord.

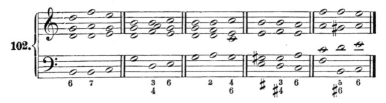

Exercises.

Note The horizontal lines in the figured bass notation indicate that the intervals next to which they are placed, have to remain stationary, while in the Bass sound the next following intervals of the chord in notation. For instance, in the first bar of the first exercise, the lines next the figures $\frac{3}{4}$ indicate, that the intervals of the triad on G—which correspond to these figures—have to sound on during the following three notes of the Bass, thus giving rise to a chord of the sixth and a chord of the $\frac{6}{4}$.

The short line below the note f sharp in the last bar of the third exercise indicate that the third of the triad (leading tone) must remain stationary, while the octave progresses downward into the seventh.

A short oblique or vertical line to a figure denotes the repetition of that figure.

CHAPTER XIV.

The connection of dissonant Harmonies resolving into the tonic triad.

§ 40. The dissonant chords just treated, need not always resolve directly into the triad. In some cases these chords are repeated once, or several times, before being resolved; or they are even led first into other dissonant chords.

Following are a few such cases:

a) The fundamental form of the Dominant chord is repeated several times, whereby complete chords must not be mingled with incomplete ones lacking the fifth.

Where the fifth is wanting, such a repetition of the chord is permitted only on condition that the seventh is never led into the fundamental tone, except when it appears in the Alto, and the chord is in close position.

In free-voice-leading the Dominant chord may be repeated in the most diverse positions, provided the seventh is never led into the fundamental.

b) In connecting the inversions of the Dominant chord with one another and with the fundamental form, the seventh should, if possible, be retained in the same voice or at least in the same octave. In certain cases it may be led into another interval of the chord; but by no means into the fundamental.

c) Repetitions of the chord of the ninth are rare; in minor they involve the exceedingly harsh step of the augmented second—from the 6-th to the 7-th degree. Often, however, the chord of the ninth is followed by the chord of the dominant-seventh, which chord-combination results from premature resolution of the ninth into the fifth of the tonic triad (at the same time fundamental tone of the Dominant chord.

d) The connection of various forms of the minor chord of the seventh with one another is allowed only, if the seventh remains in the same octave:

or, in any case, is not led into the fundamental tone.

When diverse forms of the diminished chord of the seventh follow one another, the step of the augmented second has to be avoided.

Like the chord of the ninth, the chord of the seventh on the 7-th degree may precede the Dominant chord, in which case the seventh (formerly ninth) descends one step into the fundamental tone of the Dominant chord.

e) The chords of the seventh on the 5-th and 7-th degrees may also be connected with the Dominant *triad*; the seventh must here resolve not into the fundamental tone, but into the fifth of the triad.

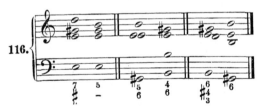

As regards the chords of the seventh on the 7-th degree, they can be connected with the Dominant *triad* only in case the latter stands between the second and third inversions of the chord of the seventh, and two voices remain stationary, while the Bass progresses in contrary motion to the third.

Exercises.

CHAPTER XV.

Chords of sequence.

§ 41. If we repeat, several times, a motive consisting of the dominant chord and the tonic triad, and descend one step with each repetition, we obtain a Sequence made up of a series of chords of the seventh, each one of which — like the initial dominant chord — finds its solution in a triad a fourth higher or a fifth lower. Such chords of the seventh, occurring chiefly in sequences, are termed *chords of sequence* *).

---

*) They are also called auxiliary chords of the seventh.

Such Sequences may also consist of inversions of the chords.

In open position.

To establish a smooth connection between these chords, we must see, that each triad have two tones in common with the following Seventh chord.

This purpose we accomplish by leading the fifth of the seventh chord one step downward into the fundamental tone of the triad. If we fail to do this, the Sequence loses much in beauty and continuity; and the frequent recurrence of so many acute dissonances can no longer be justified. There is also danger of extremely harsh concealed fifths.

One common tone suffices, where the seventh-chord is in its fundamental form and lacks the fifth.

If the third of the seventh chord lies in an inner voice, it can be led two steps downward; but only in contrary motion to the Bass.

Naturally this deviation can take place only, when chords are complete and in the fundamental form.

§ 42. However smoothly we lead the harmonic progressions in these sequences, jumps are unavoidable. The bass, in the fundamental form of chords, proceeds by jumps of fourths and fifths; but these being characteristic in that voice, are by no means unpleasant. But in addition to this we find a periodically recurring jump of a third in one of the upper voices. Now, where so many strongly dissonant chords follow in close succession, it should certainly be our aim so completely to fuse them together, that not a single jump occurs.

To accomplish this aim, we frequently permit the third of the seventh chord to remain stationary and unresolved; the result being an unbroken chain of sequence chords, each of which resolves into its successor.

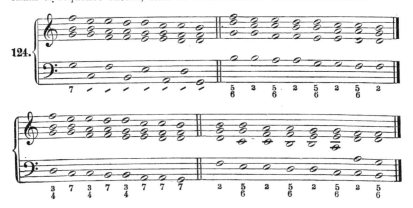

Such a sequence is but a modification of the original sequence; and the law of resolution is by no means violated, as each seventh chord contains the tones of the triad erected on its fundamental. This is illustrated in the following group of chords:

§ 43. Chords of sequence are not confined to the sequence; they may also appear otherwhere or in fragments of sequences. These fragments can be introduced by any seventh chord, we choose. We have to bear in mind, though, that the Seventh must at all times be prepared—that is, it must be contained in the same voice of the preceding chord.

If the third of a sequence chord in its fundamental form, lie in the upper voice, it may again—being no 'eading tone—progress two steps downward.

This cannot occur in the Seventh-chord on the first degree, as its third is leading tone to the triad on the 4-th degree.

The fifth may—except in a sequence—progress at will, even upwards: e. g.

§ 44. To become more familiar with the sequence chords, let us divide them into groups:

a) There are two sequence chords that consist of a major triad and a major seventh: these we find on the 1-st and 4-th degrees of the scale.

Their major seventh renders them extremely harsh, for which reason they are used less frequently than the others.

b) There are three sequence chords consisting of a minor triad and a minor seventh; they are found on the 2-nd, 3-rd and 6-th degrees of the scale.

Being less dissonant than the first group, they are used more often.

Of special significance is the Seventh chord on the 2-nd degree, a fact, which the student will comprehend later on. For the present we will say that its importance arises out of the fact that it is resolved into the Dominant triad, next to the tonic the most important chord of the scale.

c) The two forms of the chord of the seventh on the 7-th degree must be clearly distinguished. As minor seventh chord it resolves into the tonic triad; as chord of sequence, however, it progresses into the triad on the 3-rd degree.

The minor—

Seventh-chord

The Sequence—

Chord on the 7-th degree

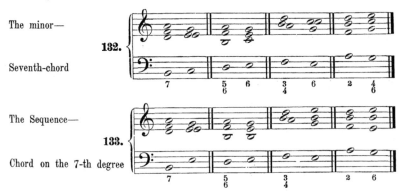

Exercises. The pupil should write out and play all the existing chords of sequence in the several major keys. Not until he has thoroughly digested the rules governing the connection and resolution of sequence chords should he work the following exercises.

*) In this chord of the sixth and fifth the seventh cannot be prepared; since, however, it has 3 tones in common with the preceding chord, no preparation is needed. Indeed, the succession of triad and chord of the seventh on the same degree always sounds good, if the triad has the fundamental doubled.

CHAPTER XVI.

Chords of sequence in minor.

§ 45. A complete sequence in minor is not practicable, since not all chords of the seventh can be resolved into the required triad or chord of the 7-th, as we shall soon see. Let us first inspect separately the chords of the seventh built on the several degrees of the minor scale.

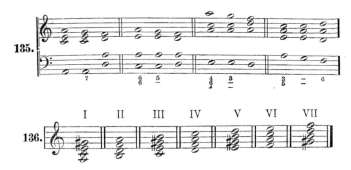

I. The chord of the seventh on the 1-st degree cannot serve our purpose, because, in its resolution, the seventh would progress downward by a tone and a half, which would be quite at variance with the real purpose of resolution. For, it is only by a *melodic* progression of the dissonance downward into a consonance, that our musical susceptibilities, disturbed by that dissonance, are quitted.

II. The chord of the seventh on the 2-nd degree resolves in the regular manner into the dominant triad, and is much used.

Equally well can it be connected with the dominant chord.

III. The chord of the seventh on the 3-rd degree is a doubly dissonant chord, because it contains, besides the seventh, an augmented triad. It is nevertheless used, its augmented fifth being led, without exception, a half-tone upwards.

Still, this chord and its inversions are but rarely employed, as the preparation of the dissonances is generally fraught with much difficulty.

IV. The chord of the seventh on the 4-th degree is commonly resolved into the chord of the diminished seventh, and not into the triad, in order, firstly, that the third should not make the steps of the augmented second, and that, secondly, when the third resolves downwards, the doubling of the fundamental (at the same time leading-tone) of the augmented triad should be avoided.

141.   Resolution into the triad   —   Resol. into the Sev. chord.

V. The chord of the seventh on the 6-th degree is likewise best resolved into the seventh-chord and not into the triad of the 2-nd degree.

Resolution into the triad   —   Resol. into the Sev. chord.

VI. The chord of the seventh on the 7-th degree is not used in the character of a sequence chord, as its resolution into the harmonies of the 3-rd degree presents many difficulties.

We learn from the aforesaid, that a complete sequence in minor is not practicable. We can construct merely fragments of such a sequence, consisting of the chords on the 6-th, 2-nd and 5-th—or of the chords on the 4-th and 7-th degrees.

Exercises.

CHAPTER XVII.

The Harmonization of a given melody.

§ 46. In the harmonization of a given melody the student is confronted by a new difficulty. Not only must he see that the harmonies are properly connected, but he must find the chords which shall best answer the demands and purpose of the melody. We cannot see from the melody itself what are the chords appropriate to it; for every tone of the melody may belong to several different chords, not all of which would answer the appropriate harmonic purpose. The mere fact that one of the notes of a melody fits into a certain chord, does not justify our application of that chord. Further, we must see that the chord demanded by the melody, be such that it can be legitimately connected with its neighbours; that the voice-leading be good; and finally, that at certain points of the melody there shall occur special harmonic formulas, such as *Cadences*.

We will now examine the circumstances, conditions and points of view that determine us in the choice of this or that chord.

§ 47. The proper use of the triads, in their fundamental form is already known to us. But the functions exercised by their inversions in the harmonization of given melodies (especially in the case of the six-four chord) we must inspect more closely.

a) The chord of the Sixth appears far more frequently than any other of the inversions; and its proper use is attended by no difficulties.

We need merely strive to use it at points, where the Bass is in contrary motion. Where the Bass is at rest, this chord sounds feeble and lifeless; especially if it be followed by the fundamental form of a triad on the same Bass tone.

145.

· b) The chord of the sixth and fourth can be effectively employed in but few cases.

These are as follows:

1) When the Bass progresses through all the intervals of the triad in succession, beginning with the fundamental tone, while the upper voices remain stationary.

146.

2) When the six-four chord stands between two triads in their fundamental form, with the Bass remaining stationary.

147.

This case may be modified by allowing the Bass of the chord following the six-four chord to progress one step up-or downwards, special care being taken that the chord-connection be very smooth.

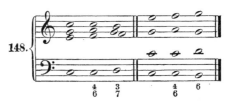

148.

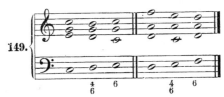

In this case the six-four chord should occur on the unaccented part of the measure.

3) When the Bass progresses stepwise into and from the chord of the sixth and fourth. The fourth is then the link between the six-four chord and the chords on either side of it. Such a case occurs for example, if the chord stands between the fundamental form and the Sixth-chord of one and the same triad,

149.

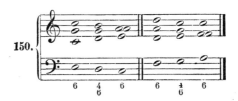

This chord must in any case be connected with one of the neighboring chords by means of its fourth; and into or from its other neighbor the fourth must progress stepwise.

150.

4) When the six-four chord occurs on the accented part of the measure, directly following its fundamental triad, and progressing into the triad a fifth above it*).

151.

There are doubtless still other opportunities for the use of the chord of the sixth and fourth; but we cannot, in a theoretical treatise, enumerate each and every case occurring in the practice of the art, the purpose of musical science being rather to contemplate and systematize the harmonic combinations in most general use.

---

*) The six-four chord is here the result of suspensions; see Chapter XXIII § 73.

It is left to the talented pupil to follow the promptings of his musical instinct and occasionally overstep the theoretical limits herein set down. The less talented student, however, who is in need of definite and concisely expressed theoretical principles should work in strict accordance with the rules, troublesome and unbending though they be. These rules have sprung empirically out of the musical promptings of man's nature.

§ 48. Let us turn now to the dissonant harmonies. The Dominant chord can be used without restriction in all cases; if its seventh is prepared the chord sounds milder and more agreeable. The resolution of the fundamental form of the Dominant chord into the tonic triad constitutes the formula called a Cadence. To this formula belongs the property of completely closing off a composition or one of its parts—especially if the triad appears in octave position. For which reason this succession of chords should be avoided in the *middle* of a piece of music. The *inversions* of the Dominant chord, however, have not this cadencing character and are therefore better suited to the intermediate portions of a piece, where the element of motion is uppermost and smooth, and fluent voice-leading necessary.

The other chords of the seventh, as well as the chord of the ninth, require preparation of their dissonances; consequently they can be employed only at points of the melody, where such preparation is possible. The diminished seventh-chord alone may enter unprepared, in the manner of the dominant chord; but good voice-leading is important. Finally, any dissonant chord can be employed, as long as a proper solution is possible.

Dissonant chords should not be used too lavishly; proper musical economy prohibits a superabundance of them. In triads lies true harmonic beauty. In his free choice of chords the beginner should not strive after exceptional, singular effect; for, while these are of inestimable value to the accomplished composer in expressing certain peculiar moods, a heaping up of vague dissonances is not advantageous in a piece of writing, which has no such special purpose, and in which absolute beauty is sought rather than relative beauty.

§ 49. We must always commence with a consonant chord in fundamental form. At the close should appear the so-called prolonged *cadence*: except in cases where the last notes of the melody exclude its use.

The augmented cadence consists of four chords, of which the last two (Dominant-seventh and Tonic) constitute the cadence, properly speaking. The first two chords must be the tonic and the subdominant. There are two kinds of prolonged cadence, depending on which of these two chords is placed first.

A. Cadences of the 1-st class are constituted as follows.

1) On an unaccented beat *) we find one of the chords belonging to the sub-dominant group—that is, either the triad on the 4-th degree (in fundamental form or as chord of the sixth) or the triad on the 2-nd degree (also in fundamental form or as chord of the sixth) or, finally, as a special exception to the rules of resolution—the chord of the seventh on the 2-nd degree, in any one of its first three forms.

2) Then follows on an accented beat the chord of the six-four of the tonic triad, which in turn is succeeded by the cadence proper, that is to say:

3) on an unaccented beat the Dominant chord or the Dominant triad and

4) on accented beat the tonic triad in its fundamental form.

Examples of prolonged cadences of the first group follow:

---

*) I must take for granted, that the distinction between accented and unaccented parts of a measure (Arsis and Thesis) is known to the pupil.

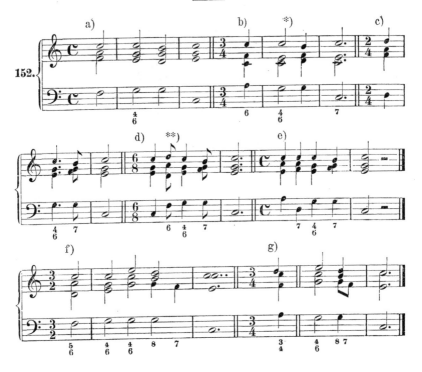

B. Cadences of *the second group* are constituted as follows.

1) On unaccented beat we find one of the chords belonging to the tonic group,—that is to say, the triads on the 1-st and 6-th degrees in fundamental form or as chord of the sixth.

2) follows on accented beat one of the chords of the sub-dominant group (triads on the 4-th or 2-nd degree or, also, the chord of the seventh on the 2-nd degree) in fundamental form or first inversion.

3) Dominant chord or Dominant triad in fundamental form.

4) the tonic triad in fundamental form.

Examples of such cadences follow:

---

*) In three-divisioned time the chord of the six-four must take up the greater part of the measure.

**) In mixed time the chord of the six-four may fall on the second accented part of the measure.

The case e, in which the chord of the sixth and fifth falls on the accented beat is one of the commonest forms of this group of cadences.

The cadence must be *perfect*; that is, the last triad must appear in the position of the octave or fifth; if this triad, however, is in the position of the third, the cadence is *imperfect*.

In minor the prolonged cadence is constructed as in major.

§ 50. We cannot sufficiently emphasize the importance of guarding from the very start against forbidden progressions of fifths and octaves. My prolonged experience has taught me, that no fault grows into a habit more easily than negligence in this respect. The ablest pupil will overlook a great number of open or concealed fifths and octaves, if he work carelessly. A closer examination of concealed progressions is here in place *).

On the whole, such progressions cannot be set down as absolute faults: there are even many cases, where they are unavoidable, e. g. in the resolution of certain dissonant chords:

Nevertheless, concealed progressions, where they are not justified by some higher harmonic law, serve to mar the purity of the writing, and are consequently to be avoided whereever possible.

Here some hints on this subject will perhaps be in place, dispelling any doubts of the student as to when and how deviations from the rules governing concealed progressions can be made.

A. Concealed octaves and fifths in the outer voices.

They are often very disagreeable and occur most frequently of all, because of the extreme mobility of these voices.

They should be avoided by all means:

---

*) These progressions are called *concealed* for the reason, that they do not actually appear in the voices in question, but must be imagined. They are hidden in the silent tones that fill out the interval of the jump made by one or both voices.

I. when the upper voice progresses by a jump *)

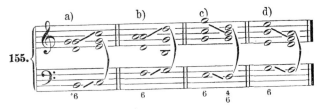

II. when all the voices progress in parallel motion.

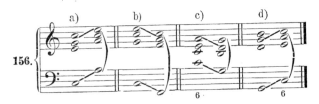

Concealed octaves sound particularly unpleasant, when the octave appears as doubled Fifth in the six-four chord, or as doubled third in the sixth—chord as in example I-c or II-d.

III. Where the outer voices move in jumps in the same direction—even though the inner voices remain stationary or progress stepwise—concealed Fifths and Octaves are likewise to be avoided.

B) Concealed progressions in the inner voices.

Concealed octaves are here entirely out of the question, arising solely in consequence of bad voice-leading

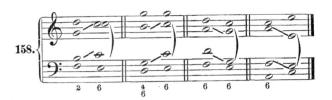

---

*) Despite the jump in the upper voice, concealed progressions sound by no means unpleasant, when they occur in the connection of a triad with the Dominant chord and when the seventh is prepared in an inner voice.

Concealed Fifths, however, are permitted, provided the voice—leading is natural.

C) Concealed progressions between an inner and outer voice are disagreeable, when the jump lies in an inner voice.

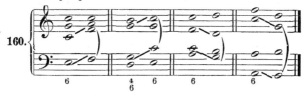

In most remaining cases concealed progressions are scarcely to be avoided (as e. g. in the resolution of the Dominant chord); and it is really not at all necessary to avoid them.

In closing this chapter we would again remind the pupil that he must concentrate his attention on good voice-leading and rational chord progressions. Only such attention will enable him entirely to avoid forbidden open progressions and to confine the use of concealed fifths and octaves to cases, where their occurrence is absolutely unavoidable *).

Note. The Bass must not progress by successive jumps in the same direction.

Jumps of sevenths—except of minor sevenths—are entirely prohibited; where the bass jumps a minor seventh, the upper voices must remain stationary.

The jump of an octave is permissible.

Exercises.

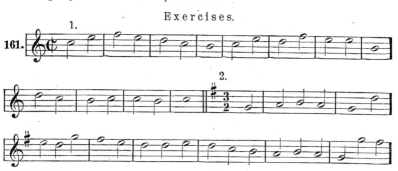

---

*) Two parallel fifths are permitted, when the second is diminished; but not vice versa.

Third Section.

Modulation.

§ 51. Harmonic combinations are not always limited to one key; they may, in the course of a composition, leave the main key, passing into the domain of neighbouring keys more or less remote and finally return to the original key.

To pass from one key into another it is not sufficient merely to employ a number of chords not belonging to the main key—we must clearly establish the new key; that is to say, we must insert a chord, that can belong only to the key we wish to reach and which, forming the bridge between the two keys, clearly defines the new from the old.

Such a transition from the harmony of one key into that of another by means of a chord, which unmistakeably denotes transition, is called: *Modulation.*

CHAPTER XVIII.

Direct Modulation.

§ 52. The quality of indicating a certain key is possessed by all dissonant chords resolving into the tonic triad; also by the dominant triad, when followed by the tonic. The most important of all modulating chords is the Dominant chord; for, notwithstanding its resolution into the tonic triad, its very outward form shows, that it can belong to but one key; which is not the case with other modulating chords. The chord of the minor seventh, for instance, while belonging to the major key on the 7-th degree of which it is erected, is also a member of the parallel minor key, on whose 2-nd degree it stands.

The Dominant chord, then, always belongs to but one key.

§ 53. Let us contemplate the modulations effected by means of this chord.

The simplest and most direct modulation would consist of but three chords; the tonic triad of the given key, the chord of the Dominant-seventh and its resolution into the tonic of the new key.

162.

The following two rules of voice-leading should be observed in order to effect a smooth connection of these three chords.

I. The Dominant-seventh chord must possess at least one tone in common with the preceding chord, which tone must be retained in the same voice.

Where the first triad has no tone in common with the following modulating chord, we must use an intermediate chord—a triad belonging either to the original key, the key to be reached, or even a key not too remotely removed from the two in question. This triad must be well connected with the original triad.

In some cases the common tones appear as harmonic alterations.

II. The two different forms of a degree, that is to say a tone and its chromatic alteration must remain in the same voice.

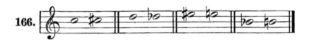

By not following this rule we obtain a very unpleasant relation between two voices; namely, the *cross-relation.*

In the following modulations cross-relations appear.

When the tone to be chromatically altered appears doubled, the effect of the cross-relation resulting is sufficiently mollified by observing the rule in one voice; a jump in the Bass is preferable to one in an upper voice.

As the Dominant-seventh chord is the same in minor as in major, the modulation remains unchanged, whether leading to major or minor. Modulations starting from minor are more difficult to effect because there are fewer intermediate chords. Resource must frequently be had to triads of other keys; in modulating half a tone downwards such a course is indeed invariably necessary.

§ 54. From the above it will be seen that, in direct modulation, correct and fluent voiceleading is the chief consideration. Jumps are permissible only in the Bass, and then not always. Jumps of augmented intervals are unmelodic; it is best to substitute them by their inversions, that is, by jumps of diminished intervals. A step of an augmented second would, for instance, have to be replaced by one of a diminished seventh.

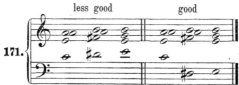

Instead of an augmented sixth use rather a diminished third.

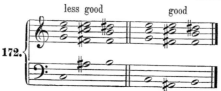

Following, are some examples of modulations from C to other keys.

1-st Exercise. Work out similar modulations from and to all the different major and minor keys.

§ 55. Modulations by means of other chords resolving into the tonic triad are subject, for the most part, to the same rules.

a) The chord of the ninth occurs but rarely as a modulating chord, since its use is always fraught with difficulty.

b) Modulations by means of the chord of the minor .seventh are also not frequent.

c) The chord of the diminished seventh is, by reason of a certain perculiarity, which we will discuss later, one of the most potent factors in modulation.

d) Modulation by means of the chord of the sixth of the diminished triad on the 7-th degree—which chord is available for modulating purposes by reason of its leading tone—is connected with some difficulty; yet it is much employed, especially in going over into neighboring keys.

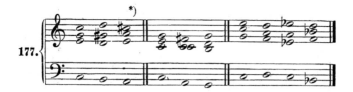

e) The Dominant triad is also used to advantage in modulating

The chords of the minor ninth and diminished seventh. while being found only in minor, are resolvable both into major and minor, which fact adapts them for purposes of modulation.

In order firmly to establish the new key and to round off the entire modulation, we employ a prolonged cadence.

*) In this modulation the chords have no common tones; but the fact that all the voices proceed stepwise sufficiently justifies their absence.

Note. All accidentals not occurring in the key must be noted in the figured bass. Instead of a sharp we often find an oblique line through the figure: *4, 6, 3, 2*; the augmented fourth is frequently expressed by 4+.

§ 56. Frequently modulation is begun by a cadence of the 1-st class. This is the case, when the six-four chord of the key to be reached is also a member of the given key.

2-nd Exercise: Work out modulations by means of the chord of the ninth, chord of the minor seventh, chord of the diminished seventh, chord of the sixth of the diminished triad, and the Dominant triad.

3-rd Exercise. Work out various modulations, using every possible time-division, and closing off each modulation by a prolonged cadence.

CHAPTER XIX.

Transient Modulation.

§ 57. Besides direct modulation, there is the indirect or transient modulation, which, instead of immediately introducing the desired key, first passes through one or more neighboring keys. It would be impossible to set down exact limits for such a degression; in general it may be said that one should choose, if not exactly the nearest-lying keys, at least such as are not too far removed from the original key. If we deviate in a direction opposite to the normal course *), we must always return to this course with the view to bring the modulation to its close.

---

*) By „normal course" I mean the circle of fifths or modulations through parallel keys.

It is furthermore impossible exactly to constitute how long we remain in any neighboring key we touch; this must be entirely left to the individual musical susceptibility of the student.

The prolonged cadence should be introduced only after the last modulation; that is, when the goal has been reached.

Following are some examples of passing modulations.

§ 58. Under this heading belongs also the transient modulation in form of a sequence. If a modulating chord be found in the motive of a sequence, it need not, in the repetition of the motive, modulate in the same direction; in this we must be governed by the degree of relationship between the chords to be connected.

Here follow some modulations in form of sequence.

In the last example we do not definitively feel the modulation until the 5-th bar, while in the preceding four bars the keys a, F, and d are barely indicated by means of the chords of the seventh on the 2-nd degree and their resolution into the respective Dominant triads.

§ 59. There are also sequences, in which every chord constitutes a modulation. They are such, in which Dominant seventh chords or other chords resolving into the tonic succeed one another, always falling a fifth or rising a fourth, as in a sequence within the limits of one key. In such a sequence, each chord resolves into a chord which itself demands resolution, and forms at the same time the resolution of its predecessor.

If we had five voices at our disposal, we could construct such a sequence, consisting of a chain of chords of the ninth resolving into one another; in four—part writing this is not practicable, since the ninth must be resolved into the fifth of the following chord; now, in a four-voiced chord of the ninth it is just the fifth, that is omitted, because no other interval can be dispensed with.

The following example shows a sequence composed purely of chords of the seventh on the 7-th degree.

All these sequences can be applied in transient modulations *).

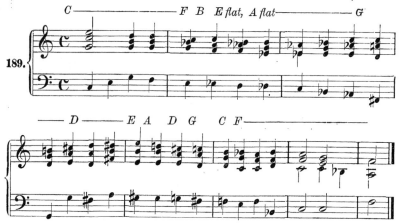

189.

Exercise: Construct numerous modulating sequences.

CHAPTER XX.

Harmonization of given melodies with modulations.

§ 60. When, in a given melody, notes occur with accidentals foreign to the key, we infer that at such points the melody modulates into some other key. What key this shall be, is determined by different circumstances. If we regard the note with the accidental as one of the intervals of the Dominant-seventh chord or some other modulating chord, we must, in choosing such a chord, see that the next note of the melody allows of its proper resolution. The choice of the chord is further conditioned by its distance from the main key.

In mere musical fragments, such as constitute the exercises of this text-book, modulations to remote keys should be avoided.

The trend of the melody itself also determines, in a measure, the choice of the modulation. If, for instance, in a melody in C major we meet with a c sharp, followed by d,—into what key would it be best to modulate? The note c sharp, coming, as it does, before d, gives us the choice between three different modulations: those into d major d minor and b minor.

191.

*) To these should be added the chain of Dominant triads.

190.

The second of those keys lies nearest, the d minor triad occurring in the key of c major. Nevertheless, we may choose either of the other two keys, provided the further tendency of the melody justifies its application.

In the first case we would have to modulate to d minor, in the second to d major, and in the third to b minor.

When, however, the melody gives no hint as to the choice of any certain key, we must follow the dictates of our musical instinct. In the following example the modulation to G is just as proper as that to E, seeing that both these keys are equally far removed from the given key.

Sometimes a modulation is called for, although there is no visible indication of it.

In the 4-th bar of the following melody, for example, the note d causes us to feel, that the modulation to e minor is to be followed by one to G major.

Finally, modulations may occur, where the melody does not really demand them.

*) At this point we encounter a modulation to a minor, which is peculiar for the fact that the chord of the seventh on the 2-nd degree resolves into the Dominant seventh chord.

Exercises.

*) Whole notes in the melody by no means demand correspondingly long notes in the other voices. The quarter notes occurring in the above melody indicate that the same time-division would be appropriate in the first two bars, and that the prolonged note in the Soprano is to be regarded merely as a tone common to several chords.

CHAPTER XXI.

The enharmonic properties of the chord of the diminished seventh.

§ 61. The diminished seventh chord consists of three minor thirds erected one on the other. In the inversions of the chord, we obtain in place of minor thirds, their enharmonic equivalents—angmented seconds. If we now substitute these augmented seconds by the corresponding minor thirds, each inversion thus enharmonically changed gives us a new diminished seventh chord.

So that every diminished seventh chord is the equivalent of three other diminished seventh chords. Twelve keys, in all, are known to us; consequently we recognize but three diminished seventh chords *distinct in sound*.

Every diminished seventh chord, then, can, by enharmonically changing its intervals, be resolved into four distinct triads.

Regarding each tone of the diminished seventh chord in turn as its seventh, we can lead this chord into four different chords of the Dominant-seventh.

We will now endeavour to use this peculiarity of the diminished seventh chord for purposes of modulation.

Exercise. Make modulations from different keys employing in each case all four resolutions of the diminished seventh chord.

CHAPTER XXII.

The Organ-point.

§ 62. When in course of a piece of music we have modulated so far from the main key that a mere prolonged cadence no longer suffices to impart to the main key its original significance, we employ the so-called *Organ-point* or *Pedal**).

This harmonic form is nothing more than a further development of the ordinary cadence of the first group. This cadence of the first group gives the feeling of a close, consisting, as it does, ot the three most important chords of the key (tonic, sub-dominant and dominant) and hence exhausting the possibilities of the entire key. Yet it does not, as we have said, suffice thoroughly to reinstate the main key, after numerous modulations into other keys have taken place. To accomplish which we must prolong the last notes of the Bass of the ordinary cadence and erect upon them diverse harmonies of the main key not found in the cadence, or even harmonies belonging to directly neighboring keys. The cadence proper consists as before, of Dominant and Tonic, while its effect is greatly intensified by these chords not in harmony with the Bass note.

An Organ-point, then, can be constructed
1) on the Dominant
2) on the Tonic.

§ 63. In the Organ-point on the Dominant there can occur besides harmonies of the main key, modulations into the key of the *Dominant, the Dominant of the Dominant,*—equivalent to the second degree and occurring mostly in minor—and the *sub-Dominant.* The Organ-point on the Dominant, being merely a prolongation of the ordinary cadence, must be introduced by the chord of the six-four of the tonic triad and closed with the triad of the 5-th degree or the Dominant seventh chord.

202.

In minor the organ point occurs more rarely. It contains a greater number of modulations and very often closes with the major triad. The permissible modulations are determined by the same considerations in minor as in major with the exception that the key of the Dominant is taken major and the key of the sub-Dominant in minor.

*) The „Pedal" of an organ is an arrangement for the reproduction of the deepest tones and consist of a sort of manual, which is played by the feet.

As the Bass of an Organ-point remains stationary, there remain, in four-part writing but three voices for the chords. The Tenor must not, however, assume the character of a Bass, but must retain the tranquil movement of an inner voice.

In triads the *fifth* is best omitted.

§ 64. In the organ-point on the tonic we may modulate into the *Dominant* (mostly in minor), into the *sub-Dominant* or into the *sub-Dominant of the sub-Dominant*—that is to say into the key lying a whole tone below the main key.

In minor the modulations remain the same, except that the sub-Dominant is usually taken minor.

The organ-point on the Dominant is frequently followed by that of the tonic.

206.

Note. The figuring of the chord-formations arising in the course of an organ-point is so complicated, that it is only in the rarest cases undertaken at all. In the figured bass of old scores we frequently find but one organ-note, under which are written the words „tasto solo“.

The organ-point on the tonic often ends in the so-called Plagal or Church-Close, which consists of the sub-dominant triad followed by the tonic triad.

207.

Exercises. Practise the construction of organ-points, especially in major. Also write passing-modulations, closing them with organ-points on dominant and tonic.

§ 65. Although the organ-point has its origin in the prolonged cadence, and hence usually occurs at the close of a composition, it is also found at the beginning or in the middle of a piece of music. In most auch cases, the organ-point is erected on the tonic, and is of short duration.

The first and last chords of these organ-points must harmonize with the bass.

§ 66. The organ-point, or pedal belongs, as its name implies, properly to the bass-voice; yet we meet with a similar harmonic formation in the upper voices, built up, as before, on one prolonged tone, and called an organ-point. Here also there can occur in the other voices chords that are not in harmony with this tone—but only where ohe voice-leading is fluent and stepwise. The first and last chords must harmonize with the prolonged note.

§ 67. Finally, there is the organ-point erected on both tonic and dominant at once; this is much employed in pieces of a pastoral character.

We wish merely to make the pupil acquainted with the organ-points shown in §§ 66 and 67; he should not attempt to make use of them in his exercises. The former of these organ-points demands more experience and skill in voice-leading than can be expected of a beginner, while the latter occurs only in operatic and symphonic compositions.

Second Part.

Accidental harmonic forms.

§ 68. Beside the recognized harmonic combinations, there occur in music tone-combinations which cannot be called chords, as they are not made up of tones systematically erected one on the other, but accidentaly arise through the melodic motion of the voices, without, however, impairing the true character of the Harmony.

Such melodic deviations of the voices from the intervals of a chord arise, when certain tones belonging to the chord do not enter simultaneonsly—as in the case of *suspensions* and *anticipations*—or when tones strange to the chord make their entrance—*passing* and *changing* notes.

First Section.

CHAPTER XXIII.

S u s p e n s i o n s.

§ 69. A suspension is the harmonic formation that arises, when not all the voices of a chord enter simultaneously; one or more of the voices enter later (are suspended), causing dissonances, which find their resolution in the chord itself.

Suspensions may be found in any of the four voices, at points, where the voice in question moves upwards or downwards by a step. We have, then,

     i. Suspensions in a downward direction,
     ii. Suspensions in an upward direction.

§ 70. The suspension downward appears where the voice progresses down by a step; this step may be either a major or a minor second. The suspension must be prepared and resolved. By the preparation of a suspension we mean that the note forming the suspension must be contained in the same voice of the preceding chord. The resolution of a suspension (since it is a dissonance) consists in leading this note one step downwards.

Consequently the suspension invariably falls on the accented beat, while its resolution occupies the beat relatively unaccented.

211.

In three-divisioned time the resolution falls on the second unaccented beat, except in cases where a new chord enters on this beat.

§ 71. Should the tone, into which the suspension would have to be resolved, be already contained in one of the three upper voices, *no suspension can take place*. The reason for this is that the musical ear tolerates the dissonance of a suspension only when it resolves into a tone which the ear positively demands, and which is not yet present in the chord. This rule is not applied to the Bass, because the presence of the tone of resolution in this voice does not hinder the resolution of the suspension.

In rare cases such an exception may also take place in the Tenor. A suspension in the upper voice of a chord of the sixth may, for instance, be resolved into a tone already contained in the tenor, if this tone represents the doubling of the fundamental or of the fifth, and if, further, the voices in question are separated by the interval of a ninth instead of a second.

§ 72. In the Bass itself suspensions occur more rarely, since, in triads in fundamental form, and in chords of the six-four, the Bass is nearly always doubled in one of the upper voices, rendering the observance of the above rule impossible.

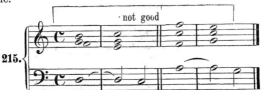

Consequently suspensions in the Bass can occur only in those rare cases, where the Bass—note is not doubled.

A suspension in the Bass sounds very good, if that voice has the third
(7-th step of the scale) of the chord.

If, however, the voice-leading demands, that the third of such a chord
be doubled, a suspension in the Bass is of course forbidden.

A suspension in the Bass is frequently found in the fundamental form
of the Dominant-seventh chord as well as in its first two inversions; in the
chord of the second, however, the suspension looses its dissonant character,
as through the suspension itself the chord of the second becomes changed
into the triad of the Dominant *).

In the other chords of the seventh—with the exception of those on the
2-nd and 7-th degrees—the suspension in the Bass sounds very harsh and is
but seldom found.

§ 73. Suspensions can also occur in two or three voices at once.

*) The suspension of the seventh does not have the effect of a suspension in any case,
even when occurring in some other voice.

The suspensions marked with crosses give rise to the sort of six-four chords of which we spoke in § 47 division 4.

Suspensions in two voices at once are permissible only when the two voices progress in parallel thirds or sixths. Parallel fourths, if not accompanied by a third voice in parallel motion, sound almost as disagreeable as parallel fifths.

§ 74. Faulty progressions are not obviated by suspensions.

Note. Before proceeding to the solution of the following exercises, a few words concerning the figuring of suspensions. In the fundamental form of triads it is sufficient to designate by figures the voice, in which the suspension is contained, though a more minute designation would not be amiss.

In the inversions of triads and in chords of the seventh both the suspension and the chord itself must be clearly designated.

Suspensions in two and three voices:

Suspensions in the Bass can be figured in two different ways: a) all the intervals that result from the suspension are indicated by figures, while under the Bass note of the resolution a horizontal line is placed; b) under the chord of resolution are written the figures properly indicating it, while oblique lines are placed under the suspension.

First mode of figuring.

Second mode.

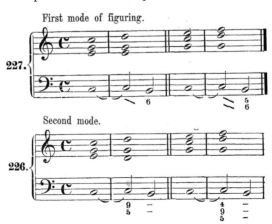

Exercises.

§ 75. 2) The suspension in an upward direction is less natural. The ear can, for the most part, tolerate a dissonance only when it progresses *downwards* into a consonance. For this reason suspensions upwards occur but seldom, and only in rare cases tend to enhance the beauty of the harmony. The suspension upwards is employed mostly at points where the leading-tone moves into the tonic.

The suspension upwards, in fact, sounds best when the voice progresses a minor second.

In the Bass this suspension is extremely rare, occurring only where the Bass-tone is not doubled in an upper voice.

§ 76. A combination of the two kinds of suspension in one and the same chord, has at times a very pleasant effect.

Exercise I.

*) In these cases neither of the two suspensions could appear separately (see rule given in § 71).

Exercise II. Harmonize the following melodies inserting many suspensions which are in turn to be most concisely figured.

§ 77. There are several exceptions to the rule governing the preparation and resolution of suspensions:

In case a) the preparation of the suspension, while appearing in the same octave, is effected by a different voice; at b) the preparation appears neither in the same voice nor in the same octave; at c) there is no preparation at all, as the suspension constitutes the first chord of a piece of music; at d) the suspension enters seemingly without preparation—this is, however, not the case, as in the bar preceding the pause the tone forming the suspension is contained in the same voice and in the same octave.

The following exceptions may occur in the resolution of suspensions.

1) Between suspension and resolution one or more notes belonging to the chord—(harmonic notes) are interposed.

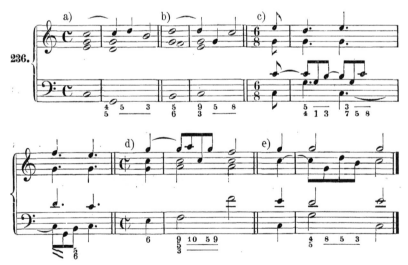

In example d) the suspended tone, before being resolved, is repeated after the harmonic notes.

2) The suspension resolves by a skip into a tone, other than the one demanded by rule: e. g.

3) While the suspension resolves in the proper way, the other voices combine to form a new chord.

The student should bear in mind these exceptional forms of suspension, even using them in his exercises, whenever his fancy or musical instinct may prompt him to do so.

Special exercises for these suspensions are superfluous.

CHAPTER XXIV.

Anticipation.

§ 78. By anticipation we mean a harmonic alteration of a chord, in which one or more of its voices adapt certain notes which really belong to the *following* chord. Anticipation, then, is the opposite of suspension, which latter, however, is far more important musically.

An anticipation must never take up an extensive part of the measure; on the contrary, the true purpose of anticipation is the enlivening of the rythm by dividing up notes of long duration.

Anticipations occur either singly, as in the last example, or in chains one after the other.

240.

A suspension and an anticipation can occur simultaneously in one and the same chord; in which case the anticipation must be of shorter duration than the suspension.

241.

§ 79. We have said that anticipation is the direct opposite of suspension; this must not, however, be taken literally, since anticipations can, for example, occur in skips, as in the case of suspensions.

242.

In anticipations our choice is not limited to any certain note of the following chord.

243.

In some cases we even employ a note, which does not actually occur in the following chord, but which might be considered part of it.

§ 80. Very similar to the anticipation is the so-called „*Cambiata*". This is a note lying one step below the preceding note of the voice and progressing by a skip downward into the nearest interval of the following chord.

§ 81. There is a syncopated movement between Bass and upper voices, which gives rise in turn to a row of suspensions or anticipations, according to whether the Bass or the upper voices fall on the accented beats.

Exercises. In the exercises the student should confine himself to the anticipations mentioned in § 78.

The other ones, as well as the cambiata he will find opportunity to employ later on.

In the harmonization of the following melodies anticipations are to be applied.

*) The note d can here be regarded as the ninth of the following chord.

CHAPTER XXV.

Passing-notes.

§ 82. Passing notes are notes not belonging to the chord which serve to fill out the intervals between two harmonic notes. According to the scale, from which they are taken, we have. I *diatonic*, II *chromatic* passing-notes.

§ 83. With diatonic passing-notes we fill out the intervals of the third and the fourth. In the third but one passing note can be inserted; in the fourth, two.

As a rule passing notes are found only on unaccented beats. They can occur in two or more voices at ance, moving either in parallel motion (in thirds or sixths), or in contrary motion. Contrary motion is preferable, since parallel progressions are in opposition to the chief element of harmonic beauty — namely an independent treatment of the voices. Nevertheless parallel progressions of passing notes in thirds and sixths need not be entirely avoided, as, if used moderately, they produce fluency and symmetry.

§ 84. Although passing notes conduce to independent voice—leading, they should not be used too copiously. If, for instance, we were to fill out every skip of a third or fourth with passing notes, we might easily fall into forbidden progressions, while such an extensive splitting up of the rythmic beats would lend the Harmony a dry pedantic character.

Such an immoderate use of passing notes is illustrated in the following bars.

Case a) shows parallel octaves. At b) two seventh occur in close succession; which is extremely unpleasant, especially in slow tempo. We should see, further, that no dissonance is formed by passing notes in contrary motion, e. g.

better so:

At c) there are parallel fifths between Tenor and Bass; at d) likewise. At e) a seventh is formed between Soprano and Bass; there are also parallel fifths. At f) a ninth is formed between Soprano and Tenor; between Soprano and Bass there are even two ninths in succession. Finally, g) shows parallel octaves.

§ 85. In minor the melodic scale is used, in order to avoid the step of the augmented second from the 6-th to the 7-th degree.

§ 86. I have said that passing notes always fall on relatively unaccented beats. To this, however, there are exceptions, of which the works of even the greatest composers show examples. This fact the student should merely bear in mind, reserving its application for more advanced exercises *).

Passing notes on accented beats occur in the following example.

*) The talented student may indeed indulge at times in exceptions to the rules, though he should not attach too much importance to such exceptional cases.

It should be remarked that it is by no means a fault, if one of two neighboring passing notes falls on a relatively accented beat.

Note. The figuring of passing notes is of no great importance, since the chord does not suffer a real change in consequence of these notes. If they are to be figured, however, not only the interval formed by the passing note, but also the entire chord must be indicated under the bass.

The following example shows the appropriate and correct application of passing notes.

Exercise. In the harmonization of the following melodies passing notes are to be employed.

§ 87. The interval of a major second is filled out by a chromatic passing note. Nothing detracts from simplicity and naturalness as much as chromatic passing notes; consequently they are to be used in moderation, and with great care.

The orthography of the chromatic scale demands sharps in ascending and flats in descending. The 6-th degree forms an exception, its sharp — in ascending—being written as the flattened 7-th degree (as at d); in like manner the flattened 5-th degree—in descending—is written as the sharp of the 4-th degree (as at c).

§ 88. In order to avoid disagreeable tone-combinations we should take care not to employ simultaneously in different voices of a chord a tone with one of its chromatic alterations, especially where that tone forms the third or the fifth of the chord.

257.

In like manner a chromatic passing note should not be used in the Bass, when the Bass tone is doubled in an upper voice.

258.

§ 89. Chromatic passing notes rarely occur in two voices at once; these also are most disagreeable, when presenting one and the same degree in its two chromatic alterations.

259.

At c) and d) we should at least write the passing notes in different form, though according to § 87 they are correct as they are.

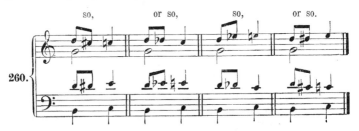

260.

In organ points chromatic passing notes in three voices produce a row of parallel chords of the sixth.

The following example shows an appropriate use of chromatic passing notes.

Exercise. Harmonize the following melodies, employing diatonic and chromatic (especially the latter) passing notes.

---

*) The orthography of the chromatic scale in minor is the same as that of the parallel major scale; the first degree forms an exception, being sharpened in ascending.

CHAPTER XXVI.
Chords of the augmented fifth.

§ 90. In consequence of the frequent recurrence of chromatic passing notes in certain cases, several such combinations of passing notes and harmonic notes have become steriotyped, and are looked upon as actual chords.

The following chords can be regarded as combinations of this sort.

I. The augmented triad.

II. The Dominant-Seventh chord with augmented fifth.

III. The chord of the seventh with the augmented fifth and major seventh.

IV. The chords of the augmented sixth.

In this chapter we shall discuss only the first three.

§ 91. I. The augmented triad is derived from the major triad by raising the fifth of the latter a half-tone. In major we can consequently have three such chords:

The augmented fifth, being here originally a chromatic passing note, must in the resolution of the chord progress half a tone upwards; accordingly the augmented triad on the tonic can resolve only into the triads of the 4-th, 2-nd and 6-th degrees.

The augmented triad on the Dominant must be resolved into the triads of the tonic, the third or the 6-th degree.

The augmented triad on the sub-dominant resolves into the triads of the 2-nd and 5-th degrees, and very rarely into that of the 7-th degree.

It can, however, also resolve into the first and third inversions of the Dominant-Seventh chord, besides certain forms of the chord of the minor seventh.

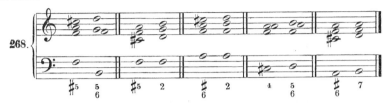

It goes without saying, that the fifth of the augmented triad can never be doubled. In most cases this triad is regarded as the Dominant of the following triad; accordingly the augmented triad on the tonic is usually found before the sub-dominant, that of the dominant before the tonic; the augmented triad on the sub-dominant modulates into the key lying a whole tone below it.

§ 92. The augmented triad must be prepared. It can be employed either as passing chord, in which case it is prepared by the original form of the triad, — or as a chord in itself, in which case it is prepared by a chord connecting smoothly with it—frequently by the same chord into which it is resolved.

The inversions of the augmented triad occur less frequently than the fundamental form; they appear mostly as passing-chords. with doubled fundamental or third.

§ 93. Of the two major triads in minor only the one of the 6-th degree is used with augmented fifth; it is subject to the general rules.

The augmented triad on the Dominant in minor is incapable of resolution.

The diatonic augmented triad of the minor scale has been mentioned in an earlier chapter.

§ 94. The augmented triad, if regarded as dominant, serves for purposes of modulation.

§ 95. Since the augmented triad consists of two major thirds erected one on the other, each triad is (as in the case of the diminished Seventh chord) the enharmonic equivalent of two other augmented triads, so that its inversions can, by enharmonic alteration of the intervals, be transformed into the fundamental form of some other augmented triad. In the same manner, the fundamental form of an augmented triad can be transformed into either one of the two inversions of two other augmented triads.

This feature of the augmented triad is also useful in modulation. If we regard each of its intervals in turn as the leading tone of the following Dominant-Seventh chord, we are enabled to make three different modulations.

Following are similar modulations with prolonged cadence added.

Exercises. Practice the preparation and resolution of augmented triads in all keys, and work out modulations by means of the enharmonic properties of these triads.

§ 96. II. The chord of the Dominant-Seventh with the augmented fifth is used only in major, and is subject to general rules; its fifth, being a chromatically altered interval, must be led a half-tone upwards. The preparation of this chord is effected by means of the triad on the 2-nd degree *).

Other chords of the key cannot be used in this capacity, as difficulties would arise in the voice-leading.

For the sake of euphony we should choose a position of this chord in which the augmented fifth lies *above* the seventh and forms with the latter interval an augmented sixth. The inverse relation of these two tones, the diminished third, is to be avoided. For which reason the second inversion of the Dominant-Seventh chord with altered fifth is not in use.

---

*) The augmented triad can also serve this purpose.

not in use.

278.

§ 97. III. The chord of the seventh with augmented fifth and major seventh is found on the 1-st and 4-th degrees, in major, and on the 6-th degree in minor. The one on the 1-st degree is most used. It is generally prepared by the tonic triad, sometimes also by the triads of the 3-rd and 5-th degrees, it is resolved into the sub-dominant triad, the altered fifth being led upwards.

oftener.

279.

Note. The chord of the seventh with augmented fifth, on the 3-rd degree in minor, has been treated in an earlier chapter.

The chord of the seventh with altered fifth on the 4-th degree in major, and that on the 6-th degree in minor occur but rarely, as their resolution is into the diminished triad. Their preparation can be effected solely by means of the triad of the 4-th degree in major and that of the 6-th degree in minor.

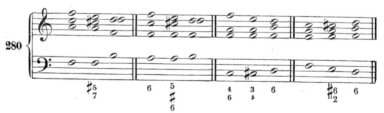

280.

Sometimes they resolve downwards by a *pure fifth* instead of by a diminished fifth and therefore modulate, from major, into the key lying a major second below the original key, from minor into the key lying a minor second above.

*) The Seventh-chord with altered fifth, on the 1-st degree is here prepared by the augmented triad of the same degree.

CHAPTER XXVII.

Chords of the augmented Sixth.

§ 98. IV. These are nothing more than the inversions of certain chords resolving into the tonic triad, and having the 2-nd degree of the scale chromatically lowered.

They are:

a) The augmented chord of the sixth (originally the first inversion of the diminished triad).

b) The augmented chord of the fourth and third (originally the second inversion of the Dominant-seventh chord).

c) The augmented chord of the sixth and fifth (originally the first inversion of the diminished seventh chord).

§ 99. a) The augmented chord of the sixth resolves into the tonic triad. It is prepared either by its original form or by the tonic triad appearing in the same position as in the resolution; the triads of the 4-th and 2-nd degrees (the latter with third doubled) can also serve.

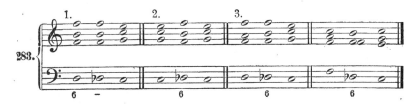

In this chord no interval except the fifth (which forms the third with the Bass) can be doubled.

§ 100. b) The augmented chord of the fourth and third is likewise resolved into the tonic triad, being prepared by the same chords, as the augmented chord of the sixth; here the fifth of the triad on the 2-nd degree may also be doubled.

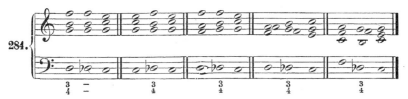

§ 101. c) In the resolution of the augmented chord of the sixth and fifth into the tonic triad parallel fifths arise.

These we can avoid in the following two ways:

A) The seventh (which forms the fifth with the Bass) undergoes a preliminary resolution into the fundamental of the Dominant-Seventh chord—as was the case in certain other resolutions—giving rise to the augmented chord of the fourth and third.

B) Two voices (the seventh and the fifth) are suspended, forming a chord of the sixth and fourth.

The augmented chord of the sixth and fifth is used either as passing chord or as an actual chord; in the former case it is prepared by its original form, in the latter by the sub-dominant triad *).

---

*) It cannot well be prepared by the triad of the 2-nd degree, as parallel fifths must necessarily occur.

§ 102. Modulations by means of the three chords just treated are permissible only, if these chords are most carefully prepared and then only, if the key to be reached is not too distant.

§ 103. These three chords nearly always resolve into major triads, since their resolution into minor (which occurs at rare intervals) does not fully satisfy the musical ear. This is probably the reason why some theorists insist upon their resolution not into the tonic but into the dominant triad and regard them as being erected not on the altered 2-nd degree, but on the altered 6-th degree, in major, and on the natural 6-th degree, in minor. According to this view we would have to consider the chords in the above examples appearing in C-major as being in F-major or F-minor, as the case demands. This would, however, be decidedly fallacious. A chord of the augmented sixth on the 6-th degree is nothing else than a modulatory degression into the key of the Dominant; this degression is indeed so unnoticeable, that without the help of a prolonged cadence we scarcely get the impression of a modulation. As soon as the resolution of this chord into the dominant triad is amplified by the insertion of a prolonged cadence, the ear feels the modulating force of the chord.

Modulatory degression—Complete modulation.

§ 104. There is still a fourth chord of the augmented sixth, which is frequently applied in cadences of the first class. This chord is found not on the 2-nd degree, but on the chromatically lowered 6-th degree; it is an augmented chord of the fourth and third with doubly augmented fourth. It is derived from the second inversion of the chord of the seventh on the 2-nd degree preceding the tonic six-four chord (*vide*; the cadence of the first class) — in consequence of chromatic passing notes in three voices *).

---

*) This chord is often confused with its enharmonic equivalent, the chord of the sixth and fifth.

§ 105. The augmented chord of the sixth and fifth is the enharmonic equivalent of the Dominant-Seventh chord of the key lying a diminished fifth below the key in question; also of the chord treated in the last paragraph, which belongs to the key of the sub-dominant.

The following modulation from C to B presents this chord in its different enharmonic forms.

§ 106. The Dominant-Seventh chord, the chord of the diminished seventh, and the doubly augmented chord of the fourth and third on the 6-th degree can occur in still other forms; the former two, for instance, with lowered second degree. These chords occur but rarely. The leading-tone must always lie above the altered interval, so that instead of a diminished third an augmented sixth is formed; or, the intervals of the diminished third must be transplanted into different octaves forming a diminished Tenth. The same applies to the inversions of the augmented chord of the fourth and third.

Exercise. Practise the preparation and resolution of the chords of the augmented sixth, and then proceed to the harmonization of the following Basses and melodies.

CHAPTER XXVIII.

Changing-notes.

§ 107. Changing notes fall on relatively unaccented beats, similarly to Passing notes, from which however they differ in that they appear between two identical harmonic notes. Every note of the chord has two changing-notes, one above and the other below.

A changing-note that is separated from its harmonic-note by a major second, may be moved closer to the harmonic note by means of an accidental. This is usually the case with the lower changing-notes; the upper changing-notes remain diatonic.

Changing-notes occurring in two voices at the same time can move either in parallel or in contrary motion. Parallel changing-notes, while having an agreeable effect, are used less frequently than those in contrary motion; the latter, though by no means always consonating, are extensively used, and, if the dissonances they form are not too harsh, contribute in a great measure to the beauty of the harmony.

Note. The figuring of changing-notes is similar to that of passing-notes (vide: note of § 86).

§ 108. By means of passing-notes and changing-notes we are enabled, while leaving the skeleton inviolate, to divide up the harmony into fragments more or less minute, thus lending the whole melodic and rythmical variety. A copious use of passing—and changing-notes in a piece constitutes *melodic figuration*, e. g.:

Note. Where crosses appear, passing—and changing-notes occur simultaneously.

Exercise. In the harmonization of the following melodies seek appropriately to employ passing—and changing notes.

§ 109. In practice changing-notes occur, deviating from the general rules, as follows:

a) changing-notes entering by a skip,

b) changing-notes on accented beats:

These changing-notes savor of the suspension, prepared as in A, unprepared as in B.

c) Two changing-notes occurring in close succession, both either on accented beat, or on unaccented beat:

---

*) At the entrance of the fourth bar we see a cross relation between Soprano and Bass, and a little further on one between Alto and Soprano; these cross relations are by no means unpleasant, since they are not formed by two harmonic notes. The d sharp in the Bass and the g sharp in the Soprano are merely changing notes entering by a skip.

303.

d) Changing-notes are often found after a suspension, sometimes even before its resolution.

304.

Here again we would advise the student not to indulge a systematic use of exceptional forms; if, in his more advanced studies, he should feel the desire to apply his knowledge of such forms, he is at liberty to do so.

§ 110. In closing this chapter we will consider briefly those accidental harmonic formations that have the *appearance* of chords. They arise on unaccented beats, when one or more voices progress in steps from chord to chord; that is, in consequence of passing or changing notes. These seeming chords can easily be distinguished from real chords by their irregular resolution, the accidental way, in which they enter, and the absence of rythmic accent.

In the following examples these accidental chords are indicated by crosses.

305.

In the following example, in which the four voices are arrayed in two groups moving in contrary motion to each-other, we find these „seeming" chords on accented beats.

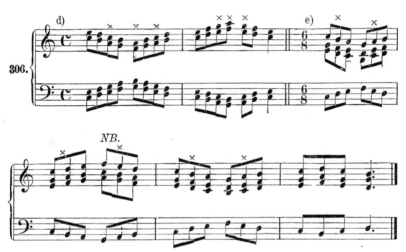

In the last example the progression in steps of all the voices justifies tone-combinations which bear not the slightest resemblance to chords. (vide: NB). Our musical instinct must aid us in determining the harmonic framework of such tone-structures; the harmonic components of example e) are about as follows:

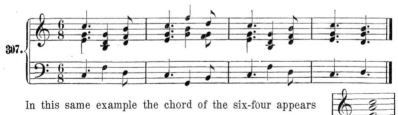

In this same example the chord of the six-four appears several times as a passing—chord.

Second Section.

The melodic development of the voices.

CHAPTER XXIX.

Strict Part—writing.

(Strenger Satz).

§ 111. Suspensions, passing-notes and changing-notes greatly enhance the melodiousness of the voices; the simplest chord—succession can, by means of these three attributes of voice-leading, be exalted to a high pitch of artistic and technical perfection. Nowhere is this perfection so thoroughly attained as in so-called *strict part-writing*. He who can skilfully handle the scanty material, to which this mode of writing is restricted, may well consider himself a master of harmonization. The seemingly insignificant material of strict part-writing coupled with a highly-finished, melodious voice-leading, enables us, after having thoroughly mastered the principles of this mode of writing, to evolve the most beautiful harmonic forms.

We have said in a former chapter that strongly dissonant tone-combinations—as, for instance, the sequence chords and the augmented and diminished chords—are frequently of great value to the composer, in cases, where, by their very harshness, he is enabled to express certain characteristic moods; these dissonances, however, possess no such significance for the student, who, uninfluenced by any special ideas or aims, seeks absolute harmonic beauty. In this sense strict partwriting is an excellent school for the young composer, since it absolutely excludes dissonance in chords, and chromatic progression in melody, pursuing chiefly the practical aim of singableness and simple intonation.

Just at this stage this strict mode of writing should prove beneficial to the student, serving as a sort of healthy contrast to the different morbid, unnatural, artificially derived harmonies, of which we have had a surfeit in the last chapters.

§ 112. Strict part-writing is founded upon a consonating relation between the Bass and the other voices; consequently it admits only major and minor triads with their first inversions, and the chord of the sixth of the diminished triad. The fourth being regarded as a dissonance, chords of the sixth and fourth are excluded. The same is true of all dissonant chords with their inversions. The cadence consists of the Dominant triad or its first inversion (the chord of the sixth of the diminished triad is also used), and its resolution into the tonic triad; the cadence must be a perfect one, that is to say, the tonic triad must appear in octave position.

308.

§ 113. Regarding the melodic progression of the voices the following should be observed: Strict part-writing admits jumps of octaves, *minor* sixths,—*pure* fifths and fourths, *major* and *minor* thirds—jumps of *major* sixths are to be avoided. Jumps of dissonant intervals (seventh) are positively prohibited—even when the notes forming them belong to the diatonic scale; chromatic progressions are likewise forbidden.

bad

§ 114. The following parallel progressions are prohibited: fifths and octaves and *major* thirds, when progressing a major second. The last restriction dates back to olden times, when music was almost entirely confined to strict part-writing, and the augmented fourth (*Tritonus*) was the only known augmented interval. Not only the Tritonus and its inversion, but any melodic and harmonic progression similar in effect, was strictly prohibited.

The parallel progression of two major thirds a *half*-tone upwards was permitted, since it gave rise to no Tritonus, e. g.

§ 115. Modulations into the nearest keys are permitted provided that chromatic progressions do not occur.

§ 116. From minor we may freely pass into the parallel major key, a modulation not being necessary; chromatic progressions are. however, to be avoided. In like manner parallel minor harmonies are permitted in major.

§ 117. For the sake of greater freedom in the voice-leading the parts may *cross*, that is to say. deviate from their normal relative position and adopt, for the time being, the inverse relation.

§ 118. From what has been said, we conclude that in strict part-writing natural intervals, that is, progressions by steps and consonant jumps are considered most singable and simple for the human voice to intonate.

Harmonic intricacies must give place to purity of intonation.

§ 119. In our exercises we shall employ the *Cantus firmus*, which, being a melody of whole notes, can easily be transposed into any other voice. We will at first harmonize this melody in whole notes, writing each voice in its respective clef, and on a separate staff.

Note. No voice must exceed its proper limits.

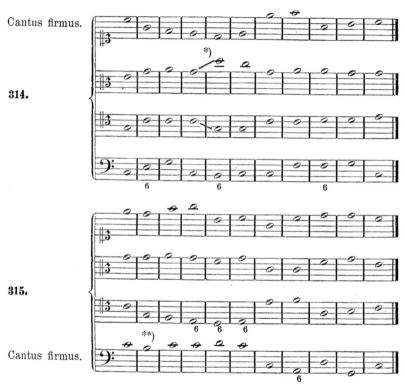

Exercise. Harmonize the following melodies, considering them as cantus firmus successively in each voice.

Note. In transposing the cantus firmus into another voice, we can employ some other key better suited to the limits of the voice in question.

§ 120. Whole notes can be split up into half notes, 1) when two different chords are to appear in the bar, 2) in consequence of suspensions, pas-

---

*) Fifths and octaves are permitted in the inner voices, if contrary motion be employed.
**) At this point the Tenor lies below the Bass, and assumes, for the time being, the significance of the latter voice.

sing and changing notes. Suspensions from above downward must be prepared and resolved according to rule. Only diatonic passing—and changing-
notes can be employed. The 7-th degree in minor is not raised when it is a
passing note.

Note. Octaves and Fifths on two similarly accented beats are regarded
as faulty open progressions.

E x e r c i s e s.

§ 121. In three-divided time two chords can appear in a bar, one
on the accented part of the measure and the other on the *second* unaccented

---

*) The exceptions to the rule governing the resolution of suspensions, as given in § 77—3,
are also permissible in strict part writing.

beat; on the first unaccented beat can appear only the resolution of a suspension, if there be one, or passing—or changing notes—no actual chord must occupy this beat.

Exercises.

§ 122. In four-divisioned time the second accented part of the measure can be occupied by an actual chord or a suspension; the unaccented beats are devoted to the resolutions of suspensions, and to passing — and changing notes.

Of the two passing-notes, which fill out the interval of a fourth, the second may fall on the second accented part of the measure (A). On this beat may also fall a changing-note following the resolution of a suspension (B). The preparation of a suspension must never be of shorter duration than the suspension itself.

In six-divisioned time two cases are to be distinguished: the six-quarter
measure and the three—half measure. In the first we have two accented
beats, the one and the *four*; in the second, however, there appear three accented beats, *one, three* and *five*. The six-quarter measure should be regarded
as consisting of two three—quarter measures: the three-half measure, as being
made up of three two—quarter measures. In the latter measure the third
and fifth quarters may be taken up by passing-notes, as in the case of the
second accented beat in four-divisioned time. A changing-note can, again,
fall on the third quarter, provided it is preceded by the resolution of a suspension. A suspended half-note can occur only at the beginning of a bar;
suspended quarter-notes can fall also on the third and fifth quarters.

324.

C. F.

*) On unaccented beat the third of the triad may be omitted.

325.

**) Here again the third of the triad is omitted on an unaccented beat.

Exercises.

§ 123. Eighth-notes occur in strict writing only in one case; namely, where a suspension on the first accented beat is followed by its resolution and the changing-note below, on the first unaccented part of the measure.

Exercises.

§ 124. In three-voiced strict writing we find either complete triads or triads with fifth omitted; in the latter the third is generally doubled. In the cadence the tonic triad can appear with third omitted.

In two-voiced writing the accented beats must be occupied by consonances, perfect or imperfect. The cadence consists either of a third whose intervals resolve by steps into the tonic prime, or of a sixth resolving into the tonic octave.

330.

Dissonances can occur, on accented beats, only in consequence of suspensions; on unaccented beats, as a result of passing—or changing-notes.

331.

Exercise. Harmonize in two and three voices a cantus firmus out of one of the preceding exercises.

§ 125. Having mastered the principles of two and three-voiced writing, we are in a position, when employing many voices, to avail ourselves from time to time of a pause in some voice. Such a pause in a voice can, however, set in only immediately after an accented beat.

Model of five-voiced writing:

332.

Model for six-voiced writing

Exercises. Harmonize several of the foregoing C. f. 's in five and six-voices.

CHAPTER XXX.

The further development of voice-leading.

Having now, in strict part-writing, learned the art, melodically to round off and perfect the voices, we can return to freer harmonic forms: all possible chord-combinations are again at our disposal, provided the elegance and fluency of the movement be not impaired, and the inordinate desire of certain chord-effects do not gain the upper hand. Strict writing is really nothing more than an excellent school; there is after all no necessity for confining ourselves to its extremely narrow limits, when so many other interesting harmonic combinations are clamoring for use. In our remaining exercises we will therefore completely reinstate all the old harmonic forms, taking care, however, not to violate the principles of melodious voice-leading. Simplicity and naturalness shall always be our aim; bold, far-fetched complications shall invariably be avoided.

Surely the student should now be competent to distinguish between harmonies that can be unreservedly employed, and those whose use is limited to certain conditions, being justified only by the distinct purpose of the composer—by the idea which underlies his composition.

For the sake of recapitulation we enumerate here the chords that constitute the essential material of Harmony:

1) All consonant triads, with their inversions.

2) The Dominant-Seventh chord and the diminished Seventh chord, with their inversions, as well as the chord of the sixth of the diminished triad.

3) The chords of sequence (whose use is, indeed, somewhat limited), of which that on the 2-nd degree is most in use.

All other chords are superfluous; at any rate their occurrence should not be too frequent, being in each case justified by a distinct purpose.

Regarding melodic figuration we would emphasize, that the suspension is first in importance. Serving as it does to animate the rythm, it presents at the same time an excellent means of chord—connection. Suspensions, moreover, impart to the harmony a refined, noble character, and supply, through their dissonance, the element of variety. They are employed to best advantage in slow movements (Andante, Adagio, Largo), since a proper appreciation of their beauty demands that the ear be clearly aware of preparation and resolution. In fast tempo, suspensions are most appropriate at the end, where the Harmony becomes more composed; here they occupy, not merely a part of the measure, but the entire measure, or even a number of measures at a time.

Passing and changing notes, while contributing nothing really new in the chords, are nevertheless of great value from a melodic and rythmic standpoint.

§ 129. Jumps, which are forbidden in strict writing, are permissible in the freer form. Of all jumps within the compass of an octave, that of the major seventh alone is unmelodic. Jumps of augmented intervals should, as we have learned, always be replaced by their inversions—diminished intervals. Chromatic progressions may occur, but not too often.

§ 130. In three—part writing the diminished triad and its second inversion may be applied.

334.

The Tritonus or its inversion may occur on accented beat in two-part writing; but only if it is followed by the tonic with third: the leading tone is led upwards into the tonic, while the 4-th degree performs a step of a second downward.

335.

To the modern musician the Tritonus does not have the force of a harsh dissonance, since it partakes of the nature of the Dominant—Seventh chord. In like manner we tolerate, in two—part writing, the minor seventh and its inversion, provided a proper resolution is effected.

336.

On the whole, all those dissonances belonging to the dominion of the Dominant-Seventh and diminished-Seventh chords are much used. The resolution into the tonic, however, must invariably follow, either directly or with the intervention of one or more intervals forming part of the dissonant chord.

337.

§ 131. The cantus firmus need not always be made up of whole notes. The following melodies are to be used as Cantus firmus in four, five, and six-part exercises.

Soprano.

338.

Alto

---

*) Special exercises in two and three-part writing are not necessary; these forms frequently occur where more voices are used during a pause of several of the voices.

§ 132. In harmonizing a voice laden with all sorts of melodic embellishments, one must carefully consider what is the proper harmony underlying each and every turn of the melody. The harmonic accompaniment of a voice so complex in structure must be characterized by rythmic tranquillity, in order, by means of contrast, better to display the melody.

Given voice.

340.

§ 133. Hitherto we have constructed our exercises within the limits of the human voice, have, that is to say, employed the vocal style, which is the surest means for mastering voice-leading — the basis of the technic of composition. The instrumental style is naturally much freer than the vocal, since it must regulate not merely a few distinct voices but great harmonic masses (Orchestre—Pianoforte—and chamber-music compositions), which only now and then give place to smaller fewer-voiced tone-combinations. Instrumental music exhibits such an infinite variety of harmonic forms, that a systematic arrangement of these were impossible. A careful analysis of standard compositions (as, for instance, the Beethoven Sonates) is the surest method for gaining a perfect comprehension of this difficult subject. For this reason the student should devote as much time as possible to the most thorough and conscientious study of the best instrumental works. A perfect comprehension of these works is however impossible without a knowledge of harmonic figuration, the subject of the following chapter.

CHAPTER XXXI.

Harmonic figuration.

§ 134. Harmonic figuration is specifically an instrumental form; in it the voices loose their individual melodic significance, and appear, in smaller rythmic divisions, as parts of one collective harmonic voice.

341.

---

*) Here an organ point can be employed, the other voices taking up the sixteenth—figures of the Bass.

In harmonic figuration we either retain the original number of melodic voices, or double each voice in a different octave — according to the range of the instrument. The laws governing the connection of harmonies must be observed in figuration; but since the ear is barely allowed time to follow the details of the chord-connection, certain irregularities (as, for instance, forbidden progressions) that are liable to occur now and then, loose their disagreeable effect.

As regards forbidden octaves, we should distinguish whether they occur in the original voices, or merely as a consequence of the doubling of one of these voices. This difference is readily seen, if we drop all repetitions of intervals, and represent the figuration in four-part writing.

The most important points in figuration are, the evolving of the *figure* or *motive*, and a conscientious application of the same.

Given harmonies.

In the repetition of the figure facility of execution must always be an important consideration; the strict application of the figure may be dispensed with in cases where playableness demands such a course.

---

*) In the given four—voiced harmonies there is no doubling of the third in this chord of the sixth; at this point however the application of the motive demands it.

In № 6 of the above examples the pianoforte is supposed to be the performing instrument; consequently the second chord (G-triad) is arranged for the left hand in a manner not representing the position of voices in the original chord of four parts. The original disposition of the parts could, in fast tempo, be difficult of execution.

345.

§ 135. If the dimensions of the motive do not permit of its full repetition on smaller divisions of the measure, the repetition of a part will suffice at these points; the rythmical movement must, however, be preserved.

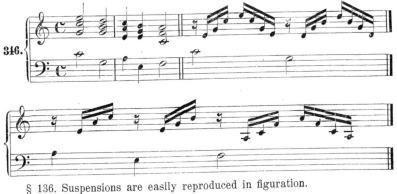

346.

§ 136. Suspensions are easily reproduced in figuration.

347.

Harmonic figuration sometimes appears in conjunction with melodic figuration. This is seen in case 5. of example 344.

Exercise. Harmonize the following Basses, employing figuration.

348.

43   98   6 $\frac{4}{6}$ 43

CHAPTER XXXII.

The free Prelude.

§ 137. A valuable exercise is the writing of free chord-progressions, dominated by no particular voice and going through all sorts of modulations.
Such exercises, which need not take any of the distinct forms recognized in
musical composition, should be characterized chiefly by skilful harmonization *). They may either end in the original key, or constitute a passing
modulation; at the close the organ-point can be employed.

349.

*) The different forms in which musical thought is presented, will become known to the
student later on.

Note. For the sake of clearness it would be advisable to employ a separate staff for each voice and to write the voices in their proper clefs.

CHAPTER XXXIII.

Deviations from the laws of Harmony.

§ 138. The laws of harmony being the outcome of experience, and corroborated as they are, by our musical instinct, are in the main incontrovertible; but in a highly-developed harmonization the melodic tendencies of the voices are so powerful, that even the boldest deviations from these laws are sometimes justified by them. The preponderance of the melodic element and the influence it exerts on chord-progression is best exhibited in the irregular resolution of dissonant harmonies.

It is obvious that a total disregard of the laws of natural chord-connection can be indulged in only by the experienced composer, who, in the pursuance of aims higher than a mere pedantic, anxious observance of rules, knowingly deviates from harmonic laws.

The Dominant-Seventh chord, for instance, would, according to the laws arising out of its very nature, have to resolve into the tonic triad; it can, however, be resolved into other triads of its own or of strange keys, provided forbidden parallel progressions and cross-relations are avoided and melodious voice-leading is observed.

The Dominant-Seventh can even resolve into a dissonant chord, provided the voice-leading is good.

In like manner every dissonant chord can resolve into a chord other than its resolution, if such a deviation be demanded by the voice-leading or the higher aims of the composer.

These irregular resolutions of dissonant chords are called: *interrupted cadences*, or *deceptive cadences*.

CHAPTER XXXIV.

Cadences (closes).

§ 139. In conclusion let us complete and systematize our knowledge of the different cadences, our treatment of which has hitherto been but fragmentary.

We have:

Complete close (authentic).
Half close and
Deceptive cadence.

The complete close consists of the harmonies of dominant and tonic. If both these chords appear in fundamental form, and the tonic triad moreover in octave position, the cadence is called *perfect*; otherwise it is termed *imperfect*.

When the fundamental (in the Bass) of the Dominant resolves into a degree other than that of the tonic, we have a deceptive cadence.

The Half-close is a full close reversed; the first chord of the Half-close is the tonic triad or some chord of the subdominant group; this is followed by the dominant-triad.

In addition to these closes there is the so-called *Plagal* or *Church close,* which was mentioned in an earlier chapter.

A further knowledge of cadences must be sought in the treatises on musical form.

A CATALOG OF SELECTED
DOVER BOOKS
IN ALL FIELDS OF INTEREST

A CATALOG OF SELECTED DOVER
BOOKS IN ALL FIELDS OF INTEREST

CONCERNING THE SPIRITUAL IN ART, Wassily Kandinsky. Pioneering work by father of abstract art. Thoughts on color theory, nature of art. Analysis of earlier masters. 12 illustrations. 80pp. of text. 5⅜ x 8½. 0-486-23411-8

CELTIC ART: The Methods of Construction, George Bain. Simple geometric techniques for making Celtic interlacements, spirals, Kells-type initials, animals, humans, etc. Over 500 illustrations. 160pp. 9 x 12. (Available in U.S. only.) 0-486-22923-8

AN ATLAS OF ANATOMY FOR ARTISTS, Fritz Schider. Most thorough reference work on art anatomy in the world. Hundreds of illustrations, including selections from works by Vesalius, Leonardo, Goya, Ingres, Michelangelo, others. 593 illustrations. 192pp. 7⅛ x 10¼. 0-486-20241-0

CELTIC HAND STROKE-BY-STROKE (Irish Half-Uncial from "The Book of Kells"): An Arthur Baker Calligraphy Manual, Arthur Baker. Complete guide to creating each letter of the alphabet in distinctive Celtic manner. Covers hand position, strokes, pens, inks, paper, more. Illustrated. 48pp. 8¼ x 11. 0-486-24336-2

EASY ORIGAMI, John Montroll. Charming collection of 32 projects (hat, cup, pelican, piano, swan, many more) specially designed for the novice origami hobbyist. Clearly illustrated easy-to-follow instructions insure that even beginning papercrafters will achieve successful results. 48pp. 8¼ x 11. 0-486-27298-2

BLOOMINGDALE'S ILLUSTRATED 1886 CATALOG: Fashions, Dry Goods and Housewares, Bloomingdale Brothers. Famed merchants' extremely rare catalog depicting about 1,700 products: clothing, housewares, firearms, dry goods, jewelry, more. Invaluable for dating, identifying vintage items. Also, copyright-free graphics for artists, designers. Co-published with Henry Ford Museum & Greenfield Village. 160pp. 8¼ x 11. 0-486-25780-0

THE ART OF WORLDLY WISDOM, Baltasar Gracian. "Think with the few and speak with the many," "Friends are a second existence," and "Be able to forget" are among this 1637 volume's 300 pithy maxims. A perfect source of mental and spiritual refreshment, it can be opened at random and appreciated either in brief or at length. 128pp. 5⅜ x 8½. 0-486-44034-6

JOHNSON'S DICTIONARY: A Modern Selection, Samuel Johnson (E. L. McAdam and George Milne, eds.). This modern version reduces the original 1755 edition's 2,300 pages of definitions and literary examples to a more manageable length, retaining the verbal pleasure and historical curiosity of the original. 480pp. 5³⁄₁₆ x 8¼. 0-486-44089-3

ADVENTURES OF HUCKLEBERRY FINN, Mark Twain, Illustrated by E. W. Kemble. A work of eternal richness and complexity, a source of ongoing critical debate, and a literary landmark, Twain's 1885 masterpiece about a barefoot boy's journey of self-discovery has enthralled readers around the world. This handsome clothbound reproduction of the first edition features all 174 of the original black-and-white illustrations. 368pp. 5⅜ x 8½. 0-486-44322-1

STICKLEY CRAFTSMAN FURNITURE CATALOGS, Gustav Stickley and L. & J. G. Stickley. Beautiful, functional furniture in two authentic catalogs from 1910. 594 illustrations, including 277 photos, show settles, rockers, armchairs, reclining chairs, bookcases, desks, tables. 183pp. 6½ x 9¼. 0-486-23838-5

AMERICAN LOCOMOTIVES IN HISTORIC PHOTOGRAPHS: 1858 to 1949, Ron Ziel (ed.). A rare collection of 126 meticulously detailed official photographs, called "builder portraits," of American locomotives that majestically chronicle the rise of steam locomotive power in America. Introduction. Detailed captions. xi+ 129pp. 9 x 12. 0-486-27393-8

AMERICA'S LIGHTHOUSES: An Illustrated History, Francis Ross Holland, Jr. Delightfully written, profusely illustrated fact-filled survey of over 200 American lighthouses since 1716. History, anecdotes, technological advances, more. 240pp. 8 x 10¾. 0-486-25576-X

TOWARDS A NEW ARCHITECTURE, Le Corbusier. Pioneering manifesto by founder of "International School." Technical and aesthetic theories, views of industry, economics, relation of form to function, "mass-production split" and much more. Profusely illustrated. 320pp. 6⅛ x 9¼. (Available in U.S. only.) 0-486-25023-7

HOW THE OTHER HALF LIVES, Jacob Riis. Famous journalistic record, exposing poverty and degradation of New York slums around 1900, by major social reformer. 100 striking and influential photographs. 233pp. 10 x 7⅞. 0-486-22012-5

FRUIT KEY AND TWIG KEY TO TREES AND SHRUBS, William M. Harlow. One of the handiest and most widely used identification aids. Fruit key covers 120 deciduous and evergreen species; twig key 160 deciduous species. Easily used. Over 300 photographs. 126pp. 5⅜ x 8½. 0-486-20511-8

COMMON BIRD SONGS, Dr. Donald J. Borror. Songs of 60 most common U.S. birds: robins, sparrows, cardinals, bluejays, finches, more—arranged in order of increasing complexity. Up to 9 variations of songs of each species.
Cassette and manual 0-486-99911-4

ORCHIDS AS HOUSE PLANTS, Rebecca Tyson Northen. Grow cattleyas and many other kinds of orchids–in a window, in a case, or under artificial light. 63 illustrations. 148pp. 5⅜ x 8½. 0-486-23261-1

MONSTER MAZES, Dave Phillips. Masterful mazes at four levels of difficulty. Avoid deadly perils and evil creatures to find magical treasures. Solutions for all 32 exciting illustrated puzzles. 48pp. 8¼ x 11. 0-486-26005-4

MOZART'S DON GIOVANNI (DOVER OPERA LIBRETTO SERIES), Wolfgang Amadeus Mozart. Introduced and translated by Ellen H. Bleiler. Standard Italian libretto, with complete English translation. Convenient and thoroughly portable–an ideal companion for reading along with a recording or the performance itself. Introduction. List of characters. Plot summary. 121pp. 5¼ x 8½. 0-486-24944-1

FRANK LLOYD WRIGHT'S DANA HOUSE, Donald Hoffmann. Pictorial essay of residential masterpiece with over 160 interior and exterior photos, plans, elevations, sketches and studies. 128pp. 9¼ x 10¾. 0-486-29120-0

THE CLARINET AND CLARINET PLAYING, David Pino. Lively, comprehensive work features suggestions about technique, musicianship, and musical interpretation, as well as guidelines for teaching, making your own reeds, and preparing for public performance. Includes an intriguing look at clarinet history. "A godsend," *The Clarinet,* Journal of the International Clarinet Society. Appendixes. 7 illus. 320pp. 5⅜ x 8½. 0-486-40270-3

HOLLYWOOD GLAMOR PORTRAITS, John Kobal (ed.). 145 photos from 1926-49. Harlow, Gable, Bogart, Bacall; 94 stars in all. Full background on photographers, technical aspects. 160pp. 8⅜ x 11¼. 0-486-23352-9

THE RAVEN AND OTHER FAVORITE POEMS, Edgar Allan Poe. Over 40 of the author's most memorable poems: "The Bells," "Ulalume," "Israfel," "To Helen," "The Conqueror Worm," "Eldorado," "Annabel Lee," many more. Alphabetic lists of titles and first lines. 64pp. 5$^{3}/_{16}$ x 8¼. 0-486-26685-0

PERSONAL MEMOIRS OF U. S. GRANT, Ulysses Simpson Grant. Intelligent, deeply moving firsthand account of Civil War campaigns, considered by many the finest military memoirs ever written. Includes letters, historic photographs, maps and more. 528pp. 6⅛ x 9¼. 0-486-28587-1

ANCIENT EGYPTIAN MATERIALS AND INDUSTRIES, A. Lucas and J. Harris. Fascinating, comprehensive, thoroughly documented text describes this ancient civilization's vast resources and the processes that incorporated them in daily life, including the use of animal products, building materials, cosmetics, perfumes and incense, fibers, glazed ware, glass and its manufacture, materials used in the mummification process, and much more. 544pp. 6⅛ x 9¼. (Available in U.S. only.) 0-486-40446-3

RUSSIAN STORIES/RUSSKIE RASSKAZY: A Dual-Language Book, edited by Gleb Struve. Twelve tales by such masters as Chekhov, Tolstoy, Dostoevsky, Pushkin, others. Excellent word-for-word English translations on facing pages, plus teaching and study aids, Russian/English vocabulary, biographical/critical introductions, more. 416pp. 5⅜ x 8½. 0-486-26244-8

PHILADELPHIA THEN AND NOW: 60 Sites Photographed in the Past and Present, Kenneth Finkel and Susan Oyama. Rare photographs of City Hall, Logan Square, Independence Hall, Betsy Ross House, other landmarks juxtaposed with contemporary views. Captures changing face of historic city. Introduction. Captions. 128pp. 8¼ x 11. 0-486-25790-8

NORTH AMERICAN INDIAN LIFE: Customs and Traditions of 23 Tribes, Elsie Clews Parsons (ed.). 27 fictionalized essays by noted anthropologists examine religion, customs, government, additional facets of life among the Winnebago, Crow, Zuni, Eskimo, other tribes. 480pp. 6⅛ x 9¼. 0-486-27377-6

TECHNICAL MANUAL AND DICTIONARY OF CLASSICAL BALLET, Gail Grant. Defines, explains, comments on steps, movements, poses and concepts. 15-page pictorial section. Basic book for student, viewer. 127pp. 5⅜ x 8½. 0-486-21843-0

THE MALE AND FEMALE FIGURE IN MOTION: 60 Classic Photographic Sequences, Eadweard Muybridge. 60 true-action photographs of men and women walking, running, climbing, bending, turning, etc., reproduced from rare 19th-century masterpiece. vi + 121pp. 9 x 12. 0-486-24745-7

ANIMALS: 1,419 Copyright-Free Illustrations of Mammals, Birds, Fish, Insects, etc., Jim Harter (ed.). Clear wood engravings present, in extremely lifelike poses, over 1,000 species of animals. One of the most extensive pictorial sourcebooks of its kind. Captions. Index. 284pp. 9 x 12. 0-486-23766-4

1001 QUESTIONS ANSWERED ABOUT THE SEASHORE, N. J. Berrill and Jacquelyn Berrill. Queries answered about dolphins, sea snails, sponges, starfish, fishes, shore birds, many others. Covers appearance, breeding, growth, feeding, much more. 305pp. 5¼ x 8¼. 0-486-23366-9

ATTRACTING BIRDS TO YOUR YARD, William J. Weber. Easy-to-follow guide offers advice on how to attract the greatest diversity of birds: birdhouses, feeders, water and waterers, much more. 96pp. 5³⁄₁₆ x 8¼. 0-486-28927-3

MEDICINAL AND OTHER USES OF NORTH AMERICAN PLANTS: A Historical Survey with Special Reference to the Eastern Indian Tribes, Charlotte Erichsen-Brown. Chronological historical citations document 500 years of usage of plants, trees, shrubs native to eastern Canada, northeastern U.S. Also complete identifying information. 343 illustrations. 544pp. 6½ x 9¼. 0-486-25951-X

STORYBOOK MAZES, Dave Phillips. 23 stories and mazes on two-page spreads: Wizard of Oz, Treasure Island, Robin Hood, etc. Solutions. 64pp. 8¼ x 11.
0-486-23628-5

AMERICAN NEGRO SONGS: 230 Folk Songs and Spirituals, Religious and Secular, John W. Work. This authoritative study traces the African influences of songs sung and played by black Americans at work, in church, and as entertainment. The author discusses the lyric significance of such songs as "Swing Low, Sweet Chariot," "John Henry," and others and offers the words and music for 230 songs. Bibliography. Index of Song Titles. 272pp. 6½ x 9¼. 0-486-40271-1

MOVIE-STAR PORTRAITS OF THE FORTIES, John Kobal (ed.). 163 glamor, studio photos of 106 stars of the 1940s: Rita Hayworth, Ava Gardner, Marlon Brando, Clark Gable, many more. 176pp. 8⅜ x 11¼. 0-486-23546-7

YEKL and THE IMPORTED BRIDEGROOM AND OTHER STORIES OF YIDDISH NEW YORK, Abraham Cahan. Film Hester Street based on *Yekl* (1896). Novel, other stories among first about Jewish immigrants on N.Y.'s East Side. 240pp. 5⅜ x 8½. 0-486-22427-9

SELECTED POEMS, Walt Whitman. Generous sampling from *Leaves of Grass*. Twenty-four poems include "I Hear America Singing," "Song of the Open Road," "I Sing the Body Electric," "When Lilacs Last in the Dooryard Bloom'd," "O Captain! My Captain!"—all reprinted from an authoritative edition. Lists of titles and first lines. 128pp. 5³⁄₁₆ x 8¼. 0-486-26878-0

SONGS OF EXPERIENCE: Facsimile Reproduction with 26 Plates in Full Color, William Blake. 26 full-color plates from a rare 1826 edition. Includes "The Tyger," "London," "Holy Thursday," and other poems. Printed text of poems. 48pp. 5¼ x 7.
0-486-24636-1

THE BEST TALES OF HOFFMANN, E. T. A. Hoffmann. 10 of Hoffmann's most important stories: "Nutcracker and the King of Mice," "The Golden Flowerpot," etc. 458pp. 5⅜ x 8½. 0-486-21793-0

THE BOOK OF TEA, Kakuzo Okakura. Minor classic of the Orient: entertaining, charming explanation, interpretation of traditional Japanese culture in terms of tea ceremony. 94pp. 5⅜ x 8½. 0-486-20070-1

FRENCH STORIES/CONTES FRANÇAIS: A Dual-Language Book, Wallace Fowlie. Ten stories by French masters, Voltaire to Camus: "Micromegas" by Voltaire; "The Atheist's Mass" by Balzac; "Minuet" by de Maupassant; "The Guest" by Camus, six more. Excellent English translations on facing pages. Also French-English vocabulary list, exercises, more. 352pp. 5⅜ x 8½. 0-486-26443-2

CHICAGO AT THE TURN OF THE CENTURY IN PHOTOGRAPHS: 122 Historic Views from the Collections of the Chicago Historical Society, Larry A. Viskochil. Rare large-format prints offer detailed views of City Hall, State Street, the Loop, Hull House, Union Station, many other landmarks, circa 1904-1913. Introduction. Captions. Maps. 144pp. 9⅜ x 12¼. 0-486-24656-6

OLD BROOKLYN IN EARLY PHOTOGRAPHS, 1865-1929, William Lee Younger. Luna Park, Gravesend race track, construction of Grand Army Plaza, moving of Hotel Brighton, etc. 157 previously unpublished photographs. 165pp. 8⅞ x 11¾. 0-486-23587-4

THE MYTHS OF THE NORTH AMERICAN INDIANS, Lewis Spence. Rich anthology of the myths and legends of the Algonquins, Iroquois, Pawnees and Sioux, prefaced by an extensive historical and ethnological commentary. 36 illustrations. 480pp. 5⅜ x 8½. 0-486-25967-6

AN ENCYCLOPEDIA OF BATTLES: Accounts of Over 1,560 Battles from 1479 B.C. to the Present, David Eggenberger. Essential details of every major battle in recorded history from the first battle of Megiddo in 1479 B.C. to Grenada in 1984. List of Battle Maps. New Appendix covering the years 1967-1984. Index. 99 illustrations. 544pp. 6½ x 9¼. 0-486-24913-1

SAILING ALONE AROUND THE WORLD, Captain Joshua Slocum. First man to sail around the world, alone, in small boat. One of great feats of seamanship told in delightful manner. 67 illustrations. 294pp. 5⅜ x 8½. 0-486-20326-3

ANARCHISM AND OTHER ESSAYS, Emma Goldman. Powerful, penetrating, prophetic essays on direct action, role of minorities, prison reform, puritan hypocrisy, violence, etc. 271pp. 5⅜ x 8½. 0-486-22484-8

MYTHS OF THE HINDUS AND BUDDHISTS, Ananda K. Coomaraswamy and Sister Nivedita. Great stories of the epics; deeds of Krishna, Shiva, taken from puranas, Vedas, folk tales; etc. 32 illustrations. 400pp. 5⅜ x 8½. 0-486-21759-0

MY BONDAGE AND MY FREEDOM, Frederick Douglass. Born a slave, Douglass became outspoken force in antislavery movement. The best of Douglass' autobiographies. Graphic description of slave life. 464pp. 5⅜ x 8½. 0-486-22457-0

FOLLOWING THE EQUATOR: A Journey Around the World, Mark Twain. Fascinating humorous account of 1897 voyage to Hawaii, Australia, India, New Zealand, etc. Ironic, bemused reports on peoples, customs, climate, flora and fauna, politics, much more. 197 illustrations. 720pp. 5⅜ x 8½. 0-486-26113-1

THE PEOPLE CALLED SHAKERS, Edward D. Andrews. Definitive study of Shakers: origins, beliefs, practices, dances, social organization, furniture and crafts, etc. 33 illustrations. 351pp. 5⅜ x 8½. 0-486-21081-2

THE MYTHS OF GREECE AND ROME, H. A. Guerber. A classic of mythology, generously illustrated, long prized for its simple, graphic, accurate retelling of the principal myths of Greece and Rome, and for its commentary on their origins and significance. With 64 illustrations by Michelangelo, Raphael, Titian, Rubens, Canova, Bernini and others. 480pp. 5⅜ x 8½. 0-486-27584-1

PSYCHOLOGY OF MUSIC, Carl E. Seashore. Classic work discusses music as a medium from psychological viewpoint. Clear treatment of physical acoustics, auditory apparatus, sound perception, development of musical skills, nature of musical feeling, host of other topics. 88 figures. 408pp. 5⅜ x 8½. 0-486-21851-1

LIFE IN ANCIENT EGYPT, Adolf Erman. Fullest, most thorough, detailed older account with much not in more recent books, domestic life, religion, magic, medicine, commerce, much more. Many illustrations reproduce tomb paintings, carvings, hieroglyphs, etc. 597pp. 5⅜ x 8½. 0-486-22632-8

SUNDIALS, Their Theory and Construction, Albert Waugh. Far and away the best, most thorough coverage of ideas, mathematics concerned, types, construction, adjusting anywhere. Simple, nontechnical treatment allows even children to build several of these dials. Over 100 illustrations. 230pp. 5⅜ x 8½. 0-486-22947-5

THEORETICAL HYDRODYNAMICS, L. M. Milne-Thomson. Classic exposition of the mathematical theory of fluid motion, applicable to both hydrodynamics and aerodynamics. Over 600 exercises. 768pp. 6⅛ x 9¼. 0-486-68970-0

OLD-TIME VIGNETTES IN FULL COLOR, Carol Belanger Grafton (ed.). Over 390 charming, often sentimental illustrations, selected from archives of Victorian graphics–pretty women posing, children playing, food, flowers, kittens and puppies, smiling cherubs, birds and butterflies, much more. All copyright-free. 48pp. 9¼ x 12¼. 0-486-27269-9

PERSPECTIVE FOR ARTISTS, Rex Vicat Cole. Depth, perspective of sky and sea, shadows, much more, not usually covered. 391 diagrams, 81 reproductions of drawings and paintings. 279pp. 5⅜ x 8½. 0-486-22487-2

DRAWING THE LIVING FIGURE, Joseph Sheppard. Innovative approach to artistic anatomy focuses on specifics of surface anatomy, rather than muscles and bones. Over 170 drawings of live models in front, back and side views, and in widely varying poses. Accompanying diagrams. 177 illustrations. Introduction. Index. 144pp. 8⅜ x11¼. 0-486-26723-7

GOTHIC AND OLD ENGLISH ALPHABETS: 100 Complete Fonts, Dan X. Solo. Add power, elegance to posters, signs, other graphics with 100 stunning copyright-free alphabets: Blackstone, Dolbey, Germania, 97 more–including many lower-case, numerals, punctuation marks. 104pp. 8⅛ x 11. 0-486-24695-7

THE BOOK OF WOOD CARVING, Charles Marshall Sayers. Finest book for beginners discusses fundamentals and offers 34 designs. "Absolutely first rate . . . well thought out and well executed."–E. J. Tangerman. 118pp. 7¾ x 10⅝. 0-486-23654-4

ILLUSTRATED CATALOG OF CIVIL WAR MILITARY GOODS: Union Army Weapons, Insignia, Uniform Accessories, and Other Equipment, Schuyler, Hartley, and Graham. Rare, profusely illustrated 1846 catalog includes Union Army uniform and dress regulations, arms and ammunition, coats, insignia, flags, swords, rifles, etc. 226 illustrations. 160pp. 9 x 12. 0-486-24939-5

WOMEN'S FASHIONS OF THE EARLY 1900s: An Unabridged Republication of "New York Fashions, 1909," National Cloak & Suit Co. Rare catalog of mail-order fashions documents women's and children's clothing styles shortly after the turn of the century. Captions offer full descriptions, prices. Invaluable resource for fashion, costume historians. Approximately 725 illustrations. 128pp. 8⅜ x 11¼. 0-486-27276-1

HOW TO DO BEADWORK, Mary White. Fundamental book on craft from simple projects to five-bead chains and woven works. 106 illustrations. 142pp. 5⅜ x 8.
0-486-20697-1

THE 1912 AND 1915 GUSTAV STICKLEY FURNITURE CATALOGS, Gustav Stickley. With over 200 detailed illustrations and descriptions, these two catalogs are essential reading and reference materials and identification guides for Stickley furniture. Captions cite materials, dimensions and prices. 112pp. 6½ x 9¼. 0-486-26676-1

EARLY AMERICAN LOCOMOTIVES, John H. White, Jr. Finest locomotive engravings from early 19th century: historical (1804–74), main-line (after 1870), special, foreign, etc. 147 plates. 142pp. 11⅜ x 8¼. 0-486-22772-3

LITTLE BOOK OF EARLY AMERICAN CRAFTS AND TRADES, Peter Stockham (ed.). 1807 children's book explains crafts and trades: baker, hatter, cooper, potter, and many others. 23 copperplate illustrations. 140pp. 4⅝ x 6.
0-486-23336-7

VICTORIAN FASHIONS AND COSTUMES FROM HARPER'S BAZAR, 1867–1898, Stella Blum (ed.). Day costumes, evening wear, sports clothes, shoes, hats, other accessories in over 1,000 detailed engravings. 320pp. 9⅜ x 12¼.
0-486-22990-4

THE LONG ISLAND RAIL ROAD IN EARLY PHOTOGRAPHS, Ron Ziel. Over 220 rare photos, informative text document origin (1844) and development of rail service on Long Island. Vintage views of early trains, locomotives, stations, passengers, crews, much more. Captions. 8⅞ x 11¾. 0-486-26301-0

VOYAGE OF THE LIBERDADE, Joshua Slocum. Great 19th-century mariner's thrilling, first-hand account of the wreck of his ship off South America, the 35-foot boat he built from the wreckage, and its remarkable voyage home. 128pp. 5⅜ x 8½.
0-486-40022-0

TEN BOOKS ON ARCHITECTURE, Vitruvius. The most important book ever written on architecture. Early Roman aesthetics, technology, classical orders, site selection, all other aspects. Morgan translation. 331pp. 5⅜ x 8½. 0-486-20645-9

THE HUMAN FIGURE IN MOTION, Eadweard Muybridge. More than 4,500 stopped-action photos, in action series, showing undraped men, women, children jumping, lying down, throwing, sitting, wrestling, carrying, etc. 390pp. 7⅞ x 10⅝.
0-486-20204-6 Clothbd.

TREES OF THE EASTERN AND CENTRAL UNITED STATES AND CANADA, William M. Harlow. Best one-volume guide to 140 trees. Full descriptions, woodlore, range, etc. Over 600 illustrations. Handy size. 288pp. 4½ x 6⅜. 0-486-20395-6

GROWING AND USING HERBS AND SPICES, Milo Miloradovich. Versatile handbook provides all the information needed for cultivation and use of all the herbs and spices available in North America. 4 illustrations. Index. Glossary. 236pp. 5⅜ x 8½.
0-486-25058-X

BIG BOOK OF MAZES AND LABYRINTHS, Walter Shepherd. 50 mazes and labyrinths in all–classical, solid, ripple, and more–in one great volume. Perfect inexpensive puzzler for clever youngsters. Full solutions. 112pp. 8⅛ x 11. 0-486-22951-3

PIANO TUNING, J. Cree Fischer. Clearest, best book for beginner, amateur. Simple repairs, raising dropped notes, tuning by easy method of flattened fifths. No previous skills needed. 4 illustrations. 201pp. 5⅜ x 8½. 0-486-23267-0

HINTS TO SINGERS, Lillian Nordica. Selecting the right teacher, developing confidence, overcoming stage fright, and many other important skills receive thoughtful discussion in this indispensible guide, written by a world-famous diva of four decades' experience. 96pp. 5⅜ x 8½. 0-486-40094-8

THE COMPLETE NONSENSE OF EDWARD LEAR, Edward Lear. All nonsense limericks, zany alphabets, Owl and Pussycat, songs, nonsense botany, etc., illustrated by Lear. Total of 320pp. 5⅜ x 8½. (Available in U.S. only.) 0-486-20167-8

VICTORIAN PARLOUR POETRY: An Annotated Anthology, Michael R. Turner. 117 gems by Longfellow, Tennyson, Browning, many lesser-known poets. "The Village Blacksmith," "Curfew Must Not Ring Tonight," "Only a Baby Small," dozens more, often difficult to find elsewhere. Index of poets, titles, first lines. xxiii + 325pp. 5⅝ x 8¼. 0-486-27044-0

DUBLINERS, James Joyce. Fifteen stories offer vivid, tightly focused observations of the lives of Dublin's poorer classes. At least one, "The Dead," is considered a masterpiece. Reprinted complete and unabridged from standard edition. 160pp. 5$\frac{3}{16}$ x 8¼. 0-486-26870-5

GREAT WEIRD TALES: 14 Stories by Lovecraft, Blackwood, Machen and Others, S. T. Joshi (ed.). 14 spellbinding tales, including "The Sin Eater," by Fiona McLeod, "The Eye Above the Mantel," by Frank Belknap Long, as well as renowned works by R. H. Barlow, Lord Dunsany, Arthur Machen, W. C. Morrow and eight other masters of the genre. 256pp. 5⅜ x 8½. (Available in U.S. only.) 0-486-40436-6

THE BOOK OF THE SACRED MAGIC OF ABRAMELIN THE MAGE, translated by S. MacGregor Mathers. Medieval manuscript of ceremonial magic. Basic document in Aleister Crowley, Golden Dawn groups. 268pp. 5⅜ x 8½. 0-486-23211-5

THE BATTLES THAT CHANGED HISTORY, Fletcher Pratt. Eminent historian profiles 16 crucial conflicts, ancient to modern, that changed the course of civilization. 352pp. 5⅜ x 8½. 0-486-41129-X

NEW RUSSIAN-ENGLISH AND ENGLISH-RUSSIAN DICTIONARY, M. A. O'Brien. This is a remarkably handy Russian dictionary, containing a surprising amount of information, including over 70,000 entries. 366pp. 4½ x 6⅛. 0-486-20208-9

NEW YORK IN THE FORTIES, Andreas Feininger. 162 brilliant photographs by the well-known photographer, formerly with *Life* magazine. Commuters, shoppers, Times Square at night, much else from city at its peak. Captions by John von Hartz. 181pp. 9¼ x 10¾. 0-486-23585-8

INDIAN SIGN LANGUAGE, William Tomkins. Over 525 signs developed by Sioux and other tribes. Written instructions and diagrams. Also 290 pictographs. 111pp. 6⅛ x 9¼. 0-486-22029-X

ANATOMY: A Complete Guide for Artists, Joseph Sheppard. A master of figure drawing shows artists how to render human anatomy convincingly. Over 460 illustrations. 224pp. 8⅜ x 11¼. 0-486-27279-6

MEDIEVAL CALLIGRAPHY: Its History and Technique, Marc Drogin. Spirited history, comprehensive instruction manual covers 13 styles (ca. 4th century through 15th). Excellent photographs; directions for duplicating medieval techniques with modern tools. 224pp. 8⅜ x 11¼. 0-486-26142-5

DRIED FLOWERS: How to Prepare Them, Sarah Whitlock and Martha Rankin. Complete instructions on how to use silica gel, meal and borax, perlite aggregate, sand and borax, glycerine and water to create attractive permanent flower arrangements. 12 illustrations. 32pp. 5⅜ x 8½. 0-486-21802-3

EASY-TO-MAKE BIRD FEEDERS FOR WOODWORKERS, Scott D. Campbell. Detailed, simple-to-use guide for designing, constructing, caring for and using feeders. Text, illustrations for 12 classic and contemporary designs. 96pp. 5⅜ x 8½.
0-486-25847-5

THE COMPLETE BOOK OF BIRDHOUSE CONSTRUCTION FOR WOOD-WORKERS, Scott D. Campbell. Detailed instructions, illustrations, tables. Also data on bird habitat and instinct patterns. Bibliography. 3 tables. 63 illustrations in 15 figures. 48pp. 5¼ x 8½. 0-486-24407-5

SCOTTISH WONDER TALES FROM MYTH AND LEGEND, Donald A. Mackenzie. 16 lively tales tell of giants rumbling down mountainsides, of a magic wand that turns stone pillars into warriors, of gods and goddesses, evil hags, powerful forces and more. 240pp. 5⅜ x 8½. 0-486-29677-6

THE HISTORY OF UNDERCLOTHES, C. Willett Cunnington and Phyllis Cunnington. Fascinating, well-documented survey covering six centuries of English undergarments, enhanced with over 100 illustrations: 12th-century laced-up bodice, footed long drawers (1795), 19th-century bustles, 19th-century corsets for men, Victorian "bust improvers," much more. 272pp. 5⅜ x 8¼. 0-486-27124-2

ARTS AND CRAFTS FURNITURE: The Complete Brooks Catalog of 1912, Brooks Manufacturing Co. Photos and detailed descriptions of more than 150 now very collectible furniture designs from the Arts and Crafts movement depict davenports, settees, buffets, desks, tables, chairs, bedsteads, dressers and more, all built of solid, quarter-sawed oak. Invaluable for students and enthusiasts of antiques, Americana and the decorative arts. 80pp. 6½ x 9¼. 0-486-27471-3

WILBUR AND ORVILLE: A Biography of the Wright Brothers, Fred Howard. Definitive, crisply written study tells the full story of the brothers' lives and work. A vividly written biography, unparalleled in scope and color, that also captures the spirit of an extraordinary era. 560pp. 6⅛ x 9¼. 0-486-40297-5

THE ARTS OF THE SAILOR: Knotting, Splicing and Ropework, Hervey Garrett Smith. Indispensable shipboard reference covers tools, basic knots and useful hitches; handsewing and canvas work, more. Over 100 illustrations. Delightful reading for sea lovers. 256pp. 5⅜ x 8½. 0-486-26440-8

FRANK LLOYD WRIGHT'S FALLINGWATER: The House and Its History, Second, Revised Edition, Donald Hoffmann. A total revision—both in text and illustrations—of the standard document on Fallingwater, the boldest, most personal architectural statement of Wright's mature years, updated with valuable new material from the recently opened Frank Lloyd Wright Archives. "Fascinating"—*The New York Times*. 116 illustrations. 128pp. 9¼ x 10¾. 0-486-27430-6

PHOTOGRAPHIC SKETCHBOOK OF THE CIVIL WAR, Alexander Gardner. 100 photos taken on field during the Civil War. Famous shots of Manassas Harper's Ferry, Lincoln, Richmond, slave pens, etc. 244pp. 10⅝ x 8¼. 0-486-22731-6

FIVE ACRES AND INDEPENDENCE, Maurice G. Kains. Great back-to-the-land classic explains basics of self-sufficient farming. The one book to get. 95 illustrations. 397pp. 5⅜ x 8½. 0-486-20974-1

A MODERN HERBAL, Margaret Grieve. Much the fullest, most exact, most useful compilation of herbal material. Gigantic alphabetical encyclopedia, from aconite to zedoary, gives botanical information, medical properties, folklore, economic uses, much else. Indispensable to serious reader. 161 illustrations. 888pp. 6½ x 9¼. 2-vol. set. (Available in U.S. only.)   Vol. I: 0-486-22798-7   Vol. II: 0-486-22799-5

HIDDEN TREASURE MAZE BOOK, Dave Phillips. Solve 34 challenging mazes accompanied by heroic tales of adventure. Evil dragons, people-eating plants, blood-thirsty giants, many more dangerous adversaries lurk at every twist and turn. 34 mazes, stories, solutions. 48pp. 8¼ x 11.   0-486-24566-7

LETTERS OF W. A. MOZART, Wolfgang A. Mozart. Remarkable letters show bawdy wit, humor, imagination, musical insights, contemporary musical world; includes some letters from Leopold Mozart. 276pp. 5⅜ x 8½.   0-486-22859-2

BASIC PRINCIPLES OF CLASSICAL BALLET, Agrippina Vaganova. Great Russian theoretician, teacher explains methods for teaching classical ballet. 118 illustrations. 175pp. 5⅜ x 8½.   0-486-22036-2

THE JUMPING FROG, Mark Twain. Revenge edition. The original story of The Celebrated Jumping Frog of Calaveras County, a hapless French translation, and Twain's hilarious "retranslation" from the French. 12 illustrations. 66pp. 5⅜ x 8½.
0-486-22686-7

BEST REMEMBERED POEMS, Martin Gardner (ed.). The 126 poems in this superb collection of 19th- and 20th-century British and American verse range from Shelley's "To a Skylark" to the impassioned "Renascence" of Edna St. Vincent Millay and to Edward Lear's whimsical "The Owl and the Pussycat." 224pp. 5⅜ x 8½.
0-486-27165-X

COMPLETE SONNETS, William Shakespeare. Over 150 exquisite poems deal with love, friendship, the tyranny of time, beauty's evanescence, death and other themes in language of remarkable power, precision and beauty. Glossary of archaic terms. 80pp. 5³⁄₁₆ x 8¼.   0-486-26686-9

HISTORIC HOMES OF THE AMERICAN PRESIDENTS, Second, Revised Edition, Irvin Haas. A traveler's guide to American Presidential homes, most open to the public, depicting and describing homes occupied by every American President from George Washington to George Bush. With visiting hours, admission charges, travel routes. 175 photographs. Index. 160pp. 8¼ x 11.   0-486-26751-2

THE WIT AND HUMOR OF OSCAR WILDE, Alvin Redman (ed.). More than 1,000 ripostes, paradoxes, wisecracks: Work is the curse of the drinking classes; I can resist everything except temptation; etc. 258pp. 5⅜ x 8½.   0-486-20602-5

SHAKESPEARE LEXICON AND QUOTATION DICTIONARY, Alexander Schmidt. Full definitions, locations, shades of meaning in every word in plays and poems. More than 50,000 exact quotations. 1,485pp. 6½ x 9¼. 2-vol. set.
Vol. 1: 0-486-22726-X   Vol. 2: 0-486-22727-8

SELECTED POEMS, Emily Dickinson. Over 100 best-known, best-loved poems by one of America's foremost poets, reprinted from authoritative early editions. No comparable edition at this price. Index of first lines. 64pp. 5³⁄₁₆ x 8¼. 0-486-26466-1

THE INSIDIOUS DR. FU-MANCHU, Sax Rohmer. The first of the popular mystery series introduces a pair of English detectives to their archnemesis, the diabolical Dr. Fu-Manchu. Flavorful atmosphere, fast-paced action, and colorful characters enliven this classic of the genre. 208pp. 5³⁄₁₆ x 8¼.   0-486-29898-1

THE MALLEUS MALEFICARUM OF KRAMER AND SPRENGER, translated by Montague Summers. Full text of most important witchhunter's "bible," used by both Catholics and Protestants. 278pp. 6⅝ x 10. 0-486-22802-9

SPANISH STORIES/CUENTOS ESPAÑOLES: A Dual-Language Book, Angel Flores (ed.). Unique format offers 13 great stories in Spanish by Cervantes, Borges, others. Faithful English translations on facing pages. 352pp. 5⅜ x 8½. 0-486-25399-6

GARDEN CITY, LONG ISLAND, IN EARLY PHOTOGRAPHS, 1869–1919, Mildred H. Smith. Handsome treasury of 118 vintage pictures, accompanied by carefully researched captions, document the Garden City Hotel fire (1899), the Vanderbilt Cup Race (1908), the first airmail flight departing from the Nassau Boulevard Aerodrome (1911), and much more. 96pp. 8⅞ x 11¾. 0-486-40669-5

OLD QUEENS, N.Y., IN EARLY PHOTOGRAPHS, Vincent F. Seyfried and William Asadorian. Over 160 rare photographs of Maspeth, Jamaica, Jackson Heights, and other areas. Vintage views of DeWitt Clinton mansion, 1939 World's Fair and more. Captions. 192pp. 8⅞ x 11. 0-486-26358-4

CAPTURED BY THE INDIANS: 15 Firsthand Accounts, 1750-1870, Frederick Drimmer. Astounding true historical accounts of grisly torture, bloody conflicts, relentless pursuits, miraculous escapes and more, by people who lived to tell the tale. 384pp. 5⅜ x 8½. 0-486-24901-8

THE WORLD'S GREAT SPEECHES (Fourth Enlarged Edition), Lewis Copeland, Lawrence W. Lamm, and Stephen J. McKenna. Nearly 300 speeches provide public speakers with a wealth of updated quotes and inspiration–from Pericles' funeral oration and William Jennings Bryan's "Cross of Gold Speech" to Malcolm X's powerful words on the Black Revolution and Earl of Spenser's tribute to his sister, Diana, Princess of Wales. 944pp. 5⅜ x 8⅜. 0-486-40903-1

THE BOOK OF THE SWORD, Sir Richard F. Burton. Great Victorian scholar/adventurer's eloquent, erudite history of the "queen of weapons"–from prehistory to early Roman Empire. Evolution and development of early swords, variations (sabre, broadsword, cutlass, scimitar, etc.), much more. 336pp. 6⅛ x 9¼. 0-486-25434-8

AUTOBIOGRAPHY: The Story of My Experiments with Truth, Mohandas K. Gandhi. Boyhood, legal studies, purification, the growth of the Satyagraha (nonviolent protest) movement. Critical, inspiring work of the man responsible for the freedom of India. 480pp. 5⅜ x 8½. (Available in U.S. only.) 0-486-24593-4

CELTIC MYTHS AND LEGENDS, T. W. Rolleston. Masterful retelling of Irish and Welsh stories and tales. Cuchulain, King Arthur, Deirdre, the Grail, many more. First paperback edition. 58 full-page illustrations. 512pp. 5⅜ x 8½. 0-486-26507-2

THE PRINCIPLES OF PSYCHOLOGY, William James. Famous long course complete, unabridged. Stream of thought, time perception, memory, experimental methods; great work decades ahead of its time. 94 figures. 1,391pp. 5⅜ x 8½. 2-vol. set.
Vol. I: 0-486-20381-6 Vol. II: 0-486-20382-4

THE WORLD AS WILL AND REPRESENTATION, Arthur Schopenhauer. Definitive English translation of Schopenhauer's life work, correcting more than 1,000 errors, omissions in earlier translations. Translated by E. F. J. Payne. Total of 1,269pp. 5⅜ x 8½. 2-vol. set. Vol. 1: 0-486-21761-2 Vol. 2: 0-486-21762-0

MAGIC AND MYSTERY IN TIBET, Madame Alexandra David-Neel. Experiences among lamas, magicians, sages, sorcerers, Bonpa wizards. A true psychic discovery. 32 illustrations. 321pp. 5⅜ x 8½. (Available in U.S. only.)　　0-486-22682-4

THE EGYPTIAN BOOK OF THE DEAD, E. A. Wallis Budge. Complete reproduction of Ani's papyrus, finest ever found. Full hieroglyphic text, interlinear transliteration, word-for-word translation, smooth translation. 533pp. 6½ x 9¼.
0-486-21866-X

HISTORIC COSTUME IN PICTURES, Braun & Schneider. Over 1,450 costumed figures in clearly detailed engravings–from dawn of civilization to end of 19th century. Captions. Many folk costumes. 256pp. 8⅜ x 11¾.　　0-486-23150-X

MATHEMATICS FOR THE NONMATHEMATICIAN, Morris Kline. Detailed, college-level treatment of mathematics in cultural and historical context, with numerous exercises. Recommended Reading Lists. Tables. Numerous figures. 641pp. 5⅜ x 8½.
0-486-24823-2

PROBABILISTIC METHODS IN THE THEORY OF STRUCTURES, Isaac Elishakoff. Well-written introduction covers the elements of the theory of probability from two or more random variables, the reliability of such multivariable structures, the theory of random function, Monte Carlo methods of treating problems incapable of exact solution, and more. Examples. 502pp. 5⅜ x 8½.　　0-486-40691-1

THE RIME OF THE ANCIENT MARINER, Gustave Doré, S. T. Coleridge. Doré's finest work; 34 plates capture moods, subtleties of poem. Flawless full-size reproductions printed on facing pages with authoritative text of poem. "Beautiful. Simply beautiful."–*Publisher's Weekly.* 77pp. 9¼ x 12.　　0-486-22305-1

SCULPTURE: Principles and Practice, Louis Slobodkin. Step-by-step approach to clay, plaster, metals, stone; classical and modern. 253 drawings, photos. 255pp. 8⅛ x 11.
0-486-22960-2

THE INFLUENCE OF SEA POWER UPON HISTORY, 1660–1783, A. T. Mahan. Influential classic of naval history and tactics still used as text in war colleges. First paperback edition. 4 maps. 24 battle plans. 640pp. 5⅜ x 8½.　　0-486-25509-3

THE STORY OF THE TITANIC AS TOLD BY ITS SURVIVORS, Jack Winocour (ed.). What it was really like. Panic, despair, shocking inefficiency, and a little heroism. More thrilling than any fictional account. 26 illustrations. 320pp. 5⅜ x 8½.
0-486-20610-6

ONE TWO THREE . . . INFINITY: Facts and Speculations of Science, George Gamow. Great physicist's fascinating, readable overview of contemporary science: number theory, relativity, fourth dimension, entropy, genes, atomic structure, much more. 128 illustrations. Index. 352pp. 5⅜ x 8½.　　0-486-25664-2

DALÍ ON MODERN ART: The Cuckolds of Antiquated Modern Art, Salvador Dalí. Influential painter skewers modern art and its practitioners. Outrageous evaluations of Picasso, Cézanne, Turner, more. 15 renderings of paintings discussed. 44 calligraphic decorations by Dalí. 96pp. 5⅜ x 8½. (Available in U.S. only.)　　0-486-29220-7

ANTIQUE PLAYING CARDS: A Pictorial History, Henry René D'Allemagne. Over 900 elaborate, decorative images from rare playing cards (14th–20th centuries): Bacchus, death, dancing dogs, hunting scenes, royal coats of arms, players cheating, much more. 96pp. 9¼ x 12¼.　　0-486-29265-7

MAKING FURNITURE MASTERPIECES: 30 Projects with Measured Drawings, Franklin H. Gottshall. Step-by-step instructions, illustrations for constructing handsome, useful pieces, among them a Sheraton desk, Chippendale chair, Spanish desk, Queen Anne table and a William and Mary dressing mirror. 224pp. 8⅛ x 11¼.
0-486-29338-6

NORTH AMERICAN INDIAN DESIGNS FOR ARTISTS AND CRAFTSPEOPLE, Eva Wilson. Over 360 authentic copyright-free designs adapted from Navajo blankets, Hopi pottery, Sioux buffalo hides, more. Geometrics, symbolic figures, plant and animal motifs, etc. 128pp. 8⅜ x 11. (Not for sale in the United Kingdom.)
0-486-25341-4

THE FOSSIL BOOK: A Record of Prehistoric Life, Patricia V. Rich et al. Profusely illustrated definitive guide covers everything from single-celled organisms and dinosaurs to birds and mammals and the interplay between climate and man. Over 1,500 illustrations. 760pp. 7½ x 10⅛.
0-486-29371-8

VICTORIAN ARCHITECTURAL DETAILS: Designs for Over 700 Stairs, Mantels, Doors, Windows, Cornices, Porches, and Other Decorative Elements, A. J. Bicknell & Company. Everything from dormer windows and piazzas to balconies and gable ornaments. Also includes elevations and floor plans for handsome, private residences and commercial structures. 80pp. 9⅜ x 12¼.
0-486-44015-X

WESTERN ISLAMIC ARCHITECTURE: A Concise Introduction, John D. Hoag. Profusely illustrated critical appraisal compares and contrasts Islamic mosques and palaces–from Spain and Egypt to other areas in the Middle East. 139 illustrations. 128pp. 6 x 9.
0-486-43760-4

CHINESE ARCHITECTURE: A Pictorial History, Liang Ssu-ch'eng. More than 240 rare photographs and drawings depict temples, pagodas, tombs, bridges, and imperial palaces comprising much of China's architectural heritage. 152 halftones, 94 diagrams. 232pp. 10¾ x 9⅞.
0-486-43999-2

THE RENAISSANCE: Studies in Art and Poetry, Walter Pater. One of the most talked-about books of the 19th century, *The Renaissance* combines scholarship and philosophy in an innovative work of cultural criticism that examines the achievements of Botticelli, Leonardo, Michelangelo, and other artists. "The holy writ of beauty."–Oscar Wilde. 160pp. 5⅜ x 8½.
0-486-44025-7

A TREATISE ON PAINTING, Leonardo da Vinci. The great Renaissance artist's practical advice on drawing and painting techniques covers anatomy, perspective, composition, light and shadow, and color. A classic of art instruction, it features 48 drawings by Nicholas Poussin and Leon Battista Alberti. 192pp. 5⅜ x 8½.
0-486-44155-5

THE MIND OF LEONARDO DA VINCI, Edward McCurdy. More than just a biography, this classic study by a distinguished historian draws upon Leonardo's extensive writings to offer numerous demonstrations of the Renaissance master's achievements, not only in sculpture and painting, but also in music, engineering, and even experimental aviation. 384pp. 5⅜ x 8½.
0-486-44142-3

WASHINGTON IRVING'S RIP VAN WINKLE, Illustrated by Arthur Rackham. Lovely prints that established artist as a leading illustrator of the time and forever etched into the popular imagination a classic of Catskill lore. 51 full-color plates. 80pp. 8⅜ x 11.
0-486-44242-X

HENSCHE ON PAINTING, John W. Robichaux. Basic painting philosophy and methodology of a great teacher, as expounded in his famous classes and workshops on Cape Cod. 7 illustrations in color on covers. 80pp. 5⅜ x 8½.
0-486-43728-0

CATALOG OF DOVER BOOKS

LIGHT AND SHADE: A Classic Approach to Three-Dimensional Drawing, Mrs. Mary P. Merrifield. Handy reference clearly demonstrates principles of light and shade by revealing effects of common daylight, sunshine, and candle or artificial light on geometrical solids. 13 plates. 64pp. 5⅜ x 8½. 0-486-44143-1

ASTROLOGY AND ASTRONOMY: A Pictorial Archive of Signs and Symbols, Ernst and Johanna Lehner. Treasure trove of stories, lore, and myth, accompanied by more than 300 rare illustrations of planets, the Milky Way, signs of the zodiac, comets, meteors, and other astronomical phenomena. 192pp. 8⅜ x 11. 0-486-43981-X

JEWELRY MAKING: Techniques for Metal, Tim McCreight. Easy-to-follow instructions and carefully executed illustrations describe tools and techniques, use of gems and enamels, wire inlay, casting, and other topics. 72 line illustrations and diagrams. 176pp. 8¼ x 10⅞. 0-486-44043-5

MAKING BIRDHOUSES: Easy and Advanced Projects, Gladstone Califf. Easy-to-follow instructions include diagrams for everything from a one-room house for bluebirds to a forty-two-room structure for purple martins. 56 plates; 4 figures. 80pp. 8¾ x 6⅜. 0-486-44183-0

LITTLE BOOK OF LOG CABINS: How to Build and Furnish Them, William S. Wicks. Handy how-to manual, with instructions and illustrations for building cabins in the Adirondack style, fireplaces, stairways, furniture, beamed ceilings, and more. 102 line drawings. 96pp. 8¾ x 6⅜. 0-486-44259-4

THE SEASONS OF AMERICA PAST, Eric Sloane. From "sugaring time" and strawberry picking to Indian summer and fall harvest, a whole year's activities described in charming prose and enhanced with 79 of the author's own illustrations. 160pp. 8¼ x 11. 0-486-44220-9

THE METROPOLIS OF TOMORROW, Hugh Ferriss. Generous, prophetic vision of the metropolis of the future, as perceived in 1929. Powerful illustrations of towering structures, wide avenues, and rooftop parks–all features in many of today's modern cities. 59 illustrations. 144pp. 8¼ x 11. 0-486-43727-2

THE PATH TO ROME, Hilaire Belloc. This 1902 memoir abounds in lively vignettes from a vanished time, recounting a pilgrimage on foot across the Alps and Apennines in order to "see all Europe which the Christian Faith has saved." 77 of the author's original line drawings complement his sparkling prose. 272pp. 5⅜ x 8½. 0-486-44001-X

THE HISTORY OF RASSELAS: Prince of Abissinia, Samuel Johnson. Distinguished English writer attacks eighteenth-century optimism and man's unrealistic estimates of what life has to offer. 112pp. 5⅜ x 8½. 0-486-44094-X

A VOYAGE TO ARCTURUS, David Lindsay. A brilliant flight of pure fancy, where wild creatures crowd the fantastic landscape and demented torturers dominate victims with their bizarre mental powers. 272pp. 5⅜ x 8½. 0-486-44198-9